Mediterranean Diet
Meal Prep
Cookbook

Easy and Healthy Recipes **You Can Meal Prep** For The Week

Lisa Rainolds

© Copyright 2020 by Lisa Rainolds - All rights reserved.

The following Book is reproduced below with the goal of providing information that is as accurate and as reliable as possible. Regardless, purchasing this Book can be seen as consent to the fact that both the publisher and the author of this book are in no way experts on the topics discussed within, and that any recommendations or suggestions made herein are for entertainment purposes only. Professionals should be consulted as needed before undertaking any of the actions endorsed herein.

This declaration is deemed fair and valid by both the American Bar Association and the Committee of Publishers Association and is legally binding throughout the United States.

Furthermore, the transmission, duplication, or reproduction of any of the following work, including precise information, will be considered an illegal act, irrespective of whether it is done electronically or in print. The legality extends to creating a secondary or tertiary copy of the work or a recorded copy and is only allowed with express written consent of the Publisher. All additional rights are reserved.

The information in the following pages is broadly considered to be a truthful and accurate account of facts, and as such any inattention, use or misuse of the information in question by the reader will render any resulting actions solely under their purview. There are no scenarios in which the publisher or the original author of this work can be in any fashion deemed liable for any hardship or damages that may befall them after undertaking the information described herein.

Additionally, the information found on the following pages is intended for informational purposes only and should thus be considered, universal. As befitting its nature, the information presented is without assurance regarding its continued validity or interim quality. Trademarks mentioned are done without written consent and can in no way be considered an endorsement from the trademark holder.

10 9 8 7 6 5 4 3 2 1

Contents

Your Free Gift	11
Introduction	15
PART 1: LIFESTYLE	21
Chapter 1: **Mediterranean diet Overview**	21
PART 2: LET'S START	31
Chapter 2: **Meal Prep 101**	31
Chapter 3: **Food Storage Solutions**	38
Chapter 4: **Getting Started with Meal Prep**	47
Chapter 5: **Mix & Match Healthy Meals**	61
PART 3: FOUR WEEKS MEAL PLAN	71
Chapter 6: **Week One**	71
Chapter 7: **Week Two**	78
Chapter 8: **Week Three**	83
Chapter 9: **Week Four**	88
Chapter 10: **Meal Plan Recipes**	93
- Breakfast	95
- Lunch	113

- Dinner 136

PART 4: BONUS RECIPES 158

- Snack 159
- Dessert 179
- Sauce 208
- Dressing 219

Conclusion 228

Measurement Conversions 229

About The Author 230

References 231

Index 232

Your FREE Gift

As a way of saying thanks for your purchase, I wanted to offer you a free bonus E-book called ***"The 10 Best Mediterranean diet Recipes To Stay Fit"***, exclusive for the readers of this book.

To get instant access just go to:

http://bit.ly/mediterranean10

Inside the book you will discover:

- **Healthiest Mediterranean recipes:** A set of 10 of the best Mediterranean recipes to stay fit I personally collected during my journey in this lifestyle.
- **Guess-free guidance:** Take the guesswork out of what to eat with detailed directions and easy-to-find ingredients.
- **Colored illustrations:** All the dishes are presented with colorful photos of the final result.

Introduction

There once was a woman who was 235 pounds, living in the heights of depression. She longed to find a diet that would help her feel alive when everything in her life pointed to sicknesses and impending early death. If you are reading this book, then you can probably relate. I am here to tell you that there is a diet that can help you feel as energized and rejuvenated as you once felt.

That's right, I'm referring to the Mediterranean Diet. The Mediterranean Diet draws inspiration from the regions surrounding the Mediterranean Sea, Greece, Italy, and Spain. These regions are populated by Christians, Jews, and Muslims. All with varying religious beliefs and eating styles. It is the variations of these eating styles that have been combined to create the Mediterranean Diet we know today.

Initially, the Med diet was exclusive to people within its region of origin. However, the diet grew in popularity as people realized far fewer people living in the Mediterranean region suffered from chronic diseases plaguing the other parts of the world. It has continued to grow in popularity and has grown to become one of the healthiest lifestyles to date.

Before you go telling yourself that it's impossible, hear me out for a second. I understand how you are feeling. I know, it can feel impossible at times to get a proper nutritional meal with all the hassles of life. How hard it can be not to simply order take out every night after a long day at work. I understand the need to get a quick meal just for the sake of eating before rushing out for a long day. I know because that woman I mentioned above was me two years ago.

But I approach you today, 74 pounds lighter, healthier and in the best mental state, I have ever been in my life. All thanks to

Meal Prepping on the Mediterranean Diet. The best part of it all was that following the diet was not only easy but also included a bunch of delicious meals with only one day of major prep per week.

So, I don't say it lightly when I say this Mediterranean Diet Meal Prep Cookbook is about to change your life. On the pages to follow I am going to walk you through step by step to show you exactly how I was able to prep delicious Mediterranean meals every week. This will enable you to achieve the same or even better results than I did.

To successfully transform your life, however, you need to understand the basics of both the Mediterranean Diet and Meal Prepping. Without this base knowledge, it is guaranteed that you will probably gas out after the first few weeks and revert to your old habits. Luckily, that's not the future I see for you. So, to avoid that from happening, I've included a simple guide on how to use this book. Let's dive into that now.

How to Use The Mediterranean diet Meal Prep Cookbook

Step One: Gain an Understanding of The Mediterranean Diet

The Mediterranean Diet may look different for every person who reads this book. We all have different eating preferences, allergies, and food intolerance levels. As such, the first step is to go through the upcoming chapter to ensure you understand the concepts behind the Mediterranean Diet. This way you can later make it your own.

Step Two: Gain an Understanding of Meal Prep

I often hear folks complain that Meal Prepping is boring. Others say they aren't interested in eating the same meal every day for the week. These statements are both far outside what proper

Meal Prep should look like. This leads me to believe that the vast majority of us do not understand the concept of Meal Prepping. As such step two is ensuring that by the end of that chapter you do.

Step Three: Take What You've Learned and Personalize It to Suit Your Needs

That's right! This cookbook is not one of those my way or nothing types of books. What got me through the last few years was ensuring that I had the flexibility to entertain guests with varying eating styles. It also helped to have that flexibility when I needed a change. This book will offer that same flexibility to you. Each week you will be offered both a vegetarian and omnivorous option for you to mix and match weeks as you please. So, feel free to use all you have learned in the informational chapters to tweak the weeks as needed.

Overview About What's in the Book

In the following chapters we will explore:

- An Overview of The Mediterranean Diet

- Meal Prep 101

- Food Storage Solutions

- How to Start Meal Prepping

- Mix & Match Healthy Meals

- 4 Weeks Meal Plan (Including Options for Both the Vegetarian & Omnivorous Lifestyle)

- Measurement Conversions

- New Healthy and Delicious Recipes You Will Love!

- Bonus Recipes...

Symbols to Be Aware of Throughout the Book

Symbol	Meaning
	Vegetarian Friendly
	Gluten-Free
	Sugar-Free
	Egg-Free
	Fish Allergy Warning
	Peanut Allergy Warning

Shellfish Allergy Warning

       Dairy Intolerance Warning

       Egg Allergy Warning

       Nut Allergy Warning

       Gluten Allergy Warning

PART 1: LIFESTYLE

Chapter 1

Mediterranean diet Overview

Most people cringe when they hear the word diet, as it is often associated with fad regimens that require you to restrict yourself for the purposes of weight loss. The Mediterranean Diet, however, refers more to the Greek meaning of being more of a general lifestyle. So, there is no counting calories, sourcing unusual or overly expensive products, or wiping your favorite foods of the grid. Rather, it's a lifestyle that focuses on developing an overall healthier mind, and body.

The Mediterranean Diet dates way back to the 1960s based on researchers' observations of the regions surrounding the Mediterranean Sea, Greece, Italy, and Spain. The research realized that the inhabitants of that region were inherently healthier when compared to Americans and northern Europeans. It was believed that this was a direct result of their diet. Hundreds of research studies later the diet has grown in popularity and is to date believed to be one of the best ways to maintain our overall health.

Guidelines & Principles

One of the things that make the Mediterranean Diet so easy to follow is that there are no strict rules for restrictions or added guilt. There is, however, a set of guiding principles regarding the types of foods you should strive to eat more of and others you should attempt to limit. Not in the sense of concrete amounts but more of a guide to help create a dietary pattern that is not only balanced but also sustainable for the foreseeable future. This means that you are free to take these guidelines and personalize to fit your preferred lifestyle.

As mentioned above, the Mediterranean Diet draws on flavors from all the countries that border the Mediterranean Sea. This results in a variety of fresh, colorful, and quality ingredients to ensure we are given the flexibility needed to not get bored. The key requirement is to simply practice the following defined principles:

1. Try to make plant-based foods your main focus. The largest portion of this diet should consist of fresh vegetables, herbs, whole grains, fruits, nuts, seeds, spices, and legumes. **You do not need to convert to vegetarianism completely if you haven't already. Simply try to center your meals around these foods.**

2. Only consume healthy fats. Think Extra Virgin Olive oil, and healthy unsaturated fats such as nuts, avocados, and seeds, to name a few.

3. If you aren't vegetarian, try to consume seafood at least twice per week. One of the main properties of seafood is that they provide heart- and brain-healthy omega-3 fatty acids. So, consider including herring, sardines, trout, mackerel, tuna, or even salmon in your meals.

4. Dairy, eggs, and poultry should be consumed in moderate amounts. You are free to consume them daily if the need arises but only in small to moderate amounts. They should never be the center or main ingredient in your

meals. Dairy will mostly be used in the form of yogurt or cheese.

5. Red meat and sweets should be consumed sparingly, if at all. These are often only enjoyed as treats. The Mediterranean Diet includes a limited amount of red meat due to its saturated fat content. Instead, opt for consuming leaner protein, such as turkey or chicken.

6. If you must drink wine, opt for red - in moderation. When consuming red wine, aim for a glass of five ounces or less per day for women and ten ounces for men.

7. Make water your beverage of choice. Aim to swap out sugary drinks for water whenever possible. Tea and coffee are okay but aim for sugar-free or with little sweeteners.

8. Try to get in some form of daily physical activity. You don't have to run out and join a gym if you don't already have a membership. But try to at least do light walking, dancing, or whatever you can to get moving each day.

9. Don't allow the rules of the diet to take over your life. Try to leave yourself enough time to enjoy time with your loved ones and share all you have learned with them.

Benefits of the Mediterranean Diet

The Mediterranean Diet has a myriad of health benefits and regardless of if it is something you are looking to cure or prevent in the first place, introducing the Med diet in your meals is undoubtedly one of the biggest steps you can take towards a better and healthier lifestyle. Below are some of the benefits of the Med diet;

High blood pressure – High blood pressure is responsible for at least 30 percent of ill- health-related deaths in the USA. Following the guidelines of a Med diet can go a long way in preventing high blood pressure which could eventually progress to the more dangerous hypertension. The Med diet is rich in substances such as calcium, potassium, and magnesium which all help to check the blood pressure while being low in sodium, an element common in the diet of people with high blood pressure.

Cardiovascular disease - Rather than consume foods like red meat, refined bread, hard liquor, and other heart-damaging foods, the Med diet promotes the consumption of foods that are healthy for the heart including seafood, whole grains, and red wine. The diet can help boost the health of your cardiovascular system. As a matter of fact, people who follow the guidelines of the Mediterranean Diet are less likely to develop cardiovascular ailments than those who do not by 30 percent. According to research, the Med diet is a lot more effective in the prevention of cardiovascular diseases when compared to a low-fat diet. It is also quite adept at increasing the levels of good cholesterol while simultaneously lowering the bad cholesterol levels to keep your heart in optimal health.

Stroke – According to a Premed study recently published in the New England Journal of Medicine, people with severe cardiovascular diseases who stuck to a Med diet experienced a 30% reduction in stroke. Also, provided you stick to its guidelines, Med diet is capable of substantially lowering the chances of ischemic stroke resulting from blood clots. This is according to the chair of neurology at North Shore University Hospital.

Alzheimer's – Generally, brain functions tend to decline as people age. While it is yet unclear how the Med diet is capable of improving brain functions, studies have demonstrated that the diet can significantly reduce the risk of mild cognitive impairment which can slowly progress into Alzheimer's. Thus, through preserving brain functions, the Med diet can reverse the impact of Alzheimer's on the brain. These positive effects are deemed possible as a result of the good cholesterol in the Mediterranean diet which helps to improve the overall health of the blood vessels in the body subsequently lowering the chances of Alzheimer's.

Type 2 Diabetes - Several studies have demonstrated that the Med diet significantly reduces the risk of type 2 diabetes in both healthy and unhealthy individuals. A UK-based study also indicated that people who follow a Med diet stand to benefit more, health-wise, than they can from a typical vegan, low-carb, high-protein, or high-fiber diet. In summary, the Mediterranean Diet has been proven to be more efficient in controlling glycemic levels, a benefit that can be associated with the high amounts of polyphenols in the diet.

Parkinson's Disease –Like in Alzheimer's, there is no clear and scientifically proven relationship between the prevention of Parkinson's disease and the Mediterranean diet. Nevertheless, it has been observed that people who follow the guidelines of the Mediterranean Diet have shown lower chances of being afflicted with Parkinson's. According to researchers, the reduced risk of Parkinson's may be a result of the fact that the Mediterranean diet generally contains lower amounts of substances that contribute to the development of Parkinson's. Inflammation and oxidative stress have also been associated with Parkinson's as causative factors and sticking to a Mediterranean diet can significantly lower the chances of these factors ever occurring in your lifetime.

Mind – In a quality of life evaluation survey of 11,000 students, carried out over a period of four years by the University of Navarra and the University of Las Palmas de Gran Canaria, participants who were on a Mediterranean diet recorded a better state of mind and overall mental well-being at the end of the study compared to the beginning of the study. Thus, it would not be farfetched to say that following the guidelines of the Mediterranean diet can lead to a better quality of life.

Obesity – According to reports from the Journal of Obesity Reviews, people who start the Mediterranean diet while still on healthy body weight are much less likely to ever become obese. In addition to this, the Journal of the American Medical Association encourages already overweight people to go on a Mediterranean diet as it can help you shed off a substantial amount of weight. However, it is important to understand that while a Mediterranean diet can be particularly helpful in staying fit and losing a few pounds, you will achieve better results if you exercise as well.

Cancer – According to a study published in the British Journal of Cancer, eating more vegetables and good fats as opposed to the regular consumption of red meat and bad fats can reduce your risk of cancer by up to 12 percent. A research conducted by Harvard University professor of cancer prevention and epidemiology also backs up this study, showing that from 26,000 Greek men and women, people who followed the Mediterranean diet had lower chances of developing any type of cancer later in life.

Longevity – Research shows that the Mediterranean diet is capable of reducing the risk of death by up to 20 percent, this is applicable across all ages. That said, if you want to live a longer and healthier life, a Mediterranean Diet is the way to go.

Agility –If you want to stay fit, strong, and healthy, then going on a Mediterranean diet will enrich you with all the nutrients you need to remain sharp and agile. Also, it is worth noting that older people who had started the Mediterranean diet when they were younger are at least 70 percent less likely to be as frail and feeble as their age mates later in life.

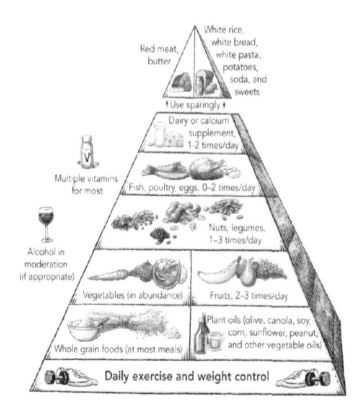

From the food pyramid above you can see that the Mediterranean diet is mostly plant-based, with seafood allowed a few times during the week, and dairy incorporated wisely on a daily or weekly basis (based on your other meals). The intake of meat and sweets should be limited to very small amounts (if at all) per month.

Having clarified what the Mediterranean Diet is, along with proof backed by scientific research on the efficiency of the Mediterranean diet as a health-improving element, it's time to learn what are the most commonly used ingredients in the diet.

Foods You Can Enjoy?

- **Oils**: extra virgin olive oil, coconut oil, and clarified butter.

- **Nuts:** walnuts, almonds, cashew nuts, and macadamia nuts.

- **Seeds:** sesame seeds, flaxseeds, and sunflower seeds.

- **Vinegar:** apple cider, red, white, and balsamic

- **Spices:** salt, garlic, black pepper, turmeric, oregano, thyme, curry, cumin, dried onion powder, mint, basil, dill, and red chili flakes.

- **Sweetener:** honey, maple syrup, molasses, agave nectar, and stevia.

- **Flours:** arrowroot powder and similar natural gluten-free flours.

- **Bread:** Sprouted grain bread also called Ezekiel bread and plain croutons.

- **Pasta:** whole wheat pasta

- **Rice:** basmati rice, wild rice, and brown rice
- **Cereal**: polenta, couscous, quinoa, and bulgur
- **Seafood:** salmon, tuna, wild-caught sardines, and other fresh seasonal fish
- **Meat**: chicken
- **Wine:** red wine
- **Vegetables:** leafy green vegetables, cabbage, carrots, tomatoes, green beans, asparagus, artichokes, onions, spinach, mushroom, cauliflower, eggplant, zucchini, and broccoli.
- **Fruits:** oranges, grapes, lemons, apples, avocados, blueberries, blackberries, raspberries, strawberries, cherries, dates, plums, figs, peaches, cantaloupes.
- **Dairy and poultry:** skim milk, eggs (cage-free), cheese, and Greek yogurt.
- **Condiments:** unsweetened ketchup, organic mayonnaise, honey mustard, tahini sauce, vinaigrette, low sodium peanut butter.
- **Snacks:** unsalted kale, unsalted crackers, hummus, nuts, fresh organic salsa, soy chips, and plain rice cakes.
- **Canned soups:** organic soups
- **Occasional treats:** healthy dark chocolate with a minimum of 70% cocoa

PART 2: LET'S START

Chapter 2

Meal Prep 101

With all our hectic schedules, we all need a healthy tool to keep us on track, and that is where Meal Prep or Meal Planning comes in. Of course, we all know that to really Meal Prep we must plan ahead, but there is truly no one method of getting it done. You will need to personalize your plan as you go along based on food preferences, cooking abilities, personal goals, and schedules.

Meal Prep Benefits

Meal Prep carries a host of benefits, including:

- **Saving Money**

Let's face it, eating out is expensive. There's the tax, tip, gas, or fare to get to the restaurant on top of the hefty cost of the food. You will save tons of cash just by eating at home. You'll also save money by planning ahead before going to the grocery store as you will be equipped with a shopping list. That's right, say bye-bye to those pesky unnecessary items that somehow always wind up in your cart, and hello to the extra dollars in the bank.

- **Saves on Food Waste**

This benefit ties in with the last. When you plan ahead on what to prepare each week, you will use what you buy. There will be no more buying too much and then having to toss out what isn't used.

- **Saving Time**

Who doesn't love quick meals after a long day? With Meal Prep you will save the time generally required to prepare meals each day. Reheating is often quick and easy.

- **Controlling Weight & Portions**

Meal Prep aids in portion control which in turn assists with losing and maintaining weight. With Meal Prep you are controlling the ingredients you choose to put in your body for every meal, giving you the power to eliminate the temptation to overeat and capitalize on necessary nutrients.

- **Eating Healthier**

By having a game plan laid out for you each week you will be afforded the flexibility of enjoying a balanced diet. As mentioned in the previous chapter, the Mediterranean Diet offers you a balanced way of eating. So, by pairing that with the concept of Meal Prep you will be giving your body the heights of nutrients of minerals each day as each meal will be intentional.

- **Getting More Done with Less Effort**

The time saved from Meal Prepping each day will open you up to a load of new opportunities and tasks that you will finally be able to complete.

- **Improving Multitasking**

The Mediterranean Diet emphasizes physical fitness and being social with friends and family. Because you'll be in the kitchen less, you'll have more time to devote to those activities. Preparing food from a prep list each week will aid in multitasking skills.

Meal Prep Principles

Many people often confuse the terms *"Meal Planning"* and *"Meal Prep"* with some even using them interchangeably. Doing so is a vital error, however, as these terms refer to two completely different concepts.

Meal Plan, as the name suggests is to plan your meals, nothing more, nothing less. It is basically you sitting down and deciding what meals you will be preparing for a given timeframe (generally a week). It involves no actual prep or additional action.

Meal Prepping, on the other hand, takes the concept and kicks it into action. It involves taking your Meal Plan and actually preparing each meal over the course of a few hours then portioning individual servings into containers to be eaten throughout the week. It is important to note, however, that it is not possible to successfully Meal Prep without first coming up with a successful Meal Plan.

As with all new things, Meal Prep can be daunting when first starting out so, don't feel bad if you need to gauge yourself in the first week. Maybe start with prepping two or three recipes to start then slowly ramp it up as the weeks go on. The speed of your journey is completely up to you, just be sure to keep the following key dos and don'ts in mind as you go forward.

Be Sure:

1. Have a Game Plan

You want to remain organized in every step of the process. So, develop a game plan. Create and use a detailed grocery list for shopping. This also includes making sure that you have the appropriate cooking equipment. Then itemize each step you need to accomplish in order before you even begin.

2. Plan for Variety

We are all creative beings that get easily bored with frequent repetition. So, ensure that you avoid boredom and change up your menu each week. A large majority of people who fail at Meal Prep merely got bored and strayed. A healthy diet consists of a variety of foods and nutrients so don't get stuck in the habit of eating the same meals each week.

3. Use Creative Recipes from Multiple Cooking Methods

Try to incorporate different cooking methods, to create a week of baked, grilled, fried, steamed stovetop, and even 'no-cook' meals. This way you can get more recipes prepared in a shorter time. As you could have something baking in the oven and another on the stovetop at the same time.

4. Batch Cook and Store Correctly

The whole purpose of Meal Prep is to create a large portion of food that will be enjoyed over an extended period of time. Proper storage after preparation goes hand in hand with food selection as without it the food you worked so hard to prepare will spill or worse spoil. To prevent this be sure to purchase airtight containers in a variety of sizes. These will lock the nutrients of your meals inside the container while keeping unwanted substances and bacteria out.

5. Portion your Meals on The Day You Prepare Them

It's easy to fall into the habit of simply transferring the prepared foods into large containers and shoving them into the refrigerator to deal with later. The issue with this is oftentimes after the fact correct portion sizes get thrown out the window as we are so tired when after a long day of work, or in such a hurry to get out the door that we end up simply tossing food onto a plate. Or worse, opting to skip the nutritious food prepared and grab fast food on the road instead, causing us to not only stray from our plan but wasting those portions that will be leftover. It's not even worth the risk. Take the extra step and portion your meals once prepared.

1. Complicated Meals

The meals you choose to prepare should be simple recipes made with easy to find ingredients that you may even already have on hand. People tend to give up on anything that proves to be more difficult than needed over time, so stick to simple recipes. Remember simple doesn't equate to boring. Simple meals can be delicious too.

2. Last-Minute Prep

Don't self-sabotage. In order for this to become sustainable, you have to come up with a workable schedule. Maybe consider preparing your list for the following week on Friday, then go shopping on Saturday so that everything will be ready and waiting to be cooked on Sunday morning. The days of the week and even your chosen structure may be different. The important thing is to have a realistic schedule and stick to it.

3. Assume You Have Enough Containers

This point cannot be stressed enough. Never start cooking until you confirm that you have enough proper containers for your food. The last thing you want is to be stuck with a large portion of spoiled food because you didn't have access to the containers you thought you had available.

4. Never Prep for More Than A Week

The rule of thumb in Meal Prep is generally to prep for a week or less. The sweet spot is between five and seven days at a time. Put bluntly your food won't last in the refrigerator forever. You want to ensure you are still getting the proper nutrients at all times and this just won't be the case if you are consuming food that is over a week old.

Types of Meal Prep

As established previously, Meal Prep is simply prepping planned meals. The most common type is individual service preparation but there are in fact various forms of Meal Prep that may be used based on your dietary needs, tastes, and schedule. Let's take a look at the different types of Meal Prep that exist.

- **Full Make-Ahead Meals**

This type of Meal Prep includes cooking and storing the entire meal as a whole in your fridge or freezer, then portioning at the time you are ready to serve.

- **Batch Cooking or Freezing**

In this method, you prepare one or more recipes in bulk that can be portioned and frozen. This approach is common for batch type recipes like mashed potatoes, soups, or rice. This is typically done for longer periods than a week.

- **Individually Portioned Meals**

This type of Meal Prep is the most common of all types. In this method, you prepare and portion your meals generally for a week.

- **Ingredient Prep**

This method of Meal Prep is perfect for people who have the time and enjoy cooking each day. In this type, all the required ingredients for the Meal Plan are prepped ahead of time and stored in individual containers to make cooking easier when the time comes.

Chapter 3

Food Storage Solutions

An important part of Meal Prep is obtaining and using the correct containers to store your food in. The selection process of your containers including size, shape, material, and ease of cleaning carries a large weight in your process.

The portability and weight also play a vital role as you will have to travel with these containers filled with food. In the same breath, investigating the quality of your storage containers. But with so many containers available on the market, how do you know what container to buy? Let's explore the various types of containers and their properties.

Container Types

Glass

BPA (Bisphenol A) is a chemical used by certain factories employed in the production of plastic. Glass containers are therefore BPA-free. They can also be durable, microwave safe, oven safe, and dishwasher approved. It does, however, come with its share of downsides. It's heavier than plastic, more expensive, and can be broken.

BPA-Free Plastic

It is of utmost importance to ensure that all plastic containers you select clearly state that the product is BPA free, microwave safe as well as dishwasher safe. Plastic containers are the most preferred when it comes to Meal Prep as they are light, airtight, and convenient.

The downside to using plastic containers, however, is that they tend to absorb the scent and in some cases color of the food they store even after washing.

Leakproof Containers/ Mason Jars

When Meal Prepping it is important to ensure that your containers and lids are airtight and leak-proof. Mason jars are perfect for storing breakfast cereals, smoothies, and anything with the potential to spill.

Selecting containers of various sizes and multiple compartments (like bento boxes) can also be used for meals in which you would like to keep the various parts separated.

Containers come in a variety of shapes and sizes. All of which will be preferred based on the dish you're prepping, or the type of Meal Prep you opt to utilize. Take, for example, a dish that has a sauce and a fried element. Storing the fried element with the sauce will cause it to get soggy and unappealing when reheated. Smoothies may refer to mason jars or smoothie cups.

Bags

Based on the meals you prepared, or the type of Meal Prep you are employing a sealable bag may be required. In the image for example a bag was used to store a batch of cookies, but it is also favored in the storage of raw or prepped ingredients.

Sometimes a bag may be most suitable for fruit or trail mix. As such sealable bags play a huge part when doing the ingredient prep method.

Freezer & Refrigerator Guidelines

Let's take a few minutes to discuss food storage guidelines, particularly for your freezer and refrigerator. I'll be the first to admit that it isn't the most glamorous part of the Meal Prep process, but it is a vital topic to cover if we want to stay safe from food-borne illness and keep our prepped food from going bad.

These guidelines include:

- Never leave food that was once chilled or cooked sitting at general room temperature for longer than two hours. General room temperature is between 40° to 90°F and is considered the 'danger zone' for these types of food. When the temperature jumps to over 90°F, the general rule of thumb drops to a maximum time of one hour. The key is to aim to keep hot foods hot and cold foods cold.

- When placing your foods inside your refrigerator, place all your uncooked meats on the bottom shelf and your cooked foods toward the top. This helps to avoid raw meat juices or blood from dripping into your already prepared foods causing cross-contamination. In the same breath, be sure to properly wrap and/or cover your foods before storing them.

- Ensure that the temperature of your refrigerator never goes over 40°F and your freezer remains at least 0°F (the freezing point).

- Consider attaching labels to your containers that you plan to store in the freezer. This could be as simple as a strip of masking tape written on with a permanent marker. This will help you to keep your freezer organized which will also aid in you standing with the freezer door open for a shorter time. By using labels, you will also be able to tag your prepared meals with a 'Cooked on date' and a 'Use by date' to lessen the chances of a meal being forgotten and going bad.

These guidelines exist because foods stored in your refrigerator and freezer can last for long time under the right conditions, but they won't last forever. The rule of thumb for perishable items is to dispose of it after a week if opened and not used.

Here is a handy chart that will guide you in knowing how long food will stay at peak quality in the refrigerator and freezer.

Food Type	Refrigerator	Freezer
RAW FISH (FRESH)	1 to 2 days	9 months
RAW POULTRY	1 to 2 days	2 to 3 months
UNCOOKED TOFU	7 days	5 months
COOKED DISHES WITH MEAT, EGGS, POULTRY, OR FISH	3 to 4 days	2 to 3 months
SOUPS & STEWS	3 to 4 days	2 to 3 months
COOKED BEANS	6 to 7 days	6 to 12 months
COOKED GRAINS	4 to 6 days	6 months
PLAIN YOGURT	1 to 2 weeks (to be eaten as is)	1 to 2 months (for smoothies or baking ONLY)
SALADS: EGG, PASTA, CHICKEN, FISH	3 to 4 days	Not recommended
HARD-COOKED EGGS	7 days	Not recommended
MUFFINS	3 to 7 days in the pantry	2 to 3 months

Reheating and Thawing Guidelines

Another set of guidelines that we must commit to memory is the concept and rules for properly thawing and reheating your food. Don't worry, there is not a lot but learning them will greatly improve the ease of your Meal Prep journey. So, let's dive into how to properly thaw frozen food.

Guidelines for Properly Thawing & Reheating Frozen Food

Never:

- Thaw your food by leaving it sitting out at room temperature. Remember the danger zone! When you do this your food will drop to a surface temperature of 40°F before the center of your food even begins to thaw. Once this happens your food will build bacteria and go bad.
- Refreeze thawed foods unless completely cooked before going back into the freezer.

Always:

- Thaw your frozen meals in the refrigerator ahead of time (generally 24 hours). This will ensure that your food maintains a 40°F temperature or less. This is the preferred method of thawing.
- Thaw under cold running water.
    - Be sure that the water remains at 70°F or lower in temperature.

- For prepared meals be sure that no part of your food goes above 40°F.

- Raw fish, poultry, or meat should maintain a surface temperature (the outside of the item) goes above 40°F while thawing for more than 4 hours.

- Defrost your foods in a microwave or toaster oven IF THE FOOD WILL BE SERVED IMMEDIATELY AFTER THAWING. This will also reheat your food so have a thermometer handy to be sure that the center of the dish gets to a safe 160°F before eating.

Top 5 Meal Prep Helpful Apps

We live in a world that has become very 'productivity' and 'to-do list' focused and the act of Meal Planning/prepping is no different. The truth is that creating proper Meal Plans with healthy means takes research time and energy that many of us may not have. Luckily, there are mobile apps that can automate the process of tailoring a plan to suit your tastes and nutritional needs.

Here are the top 5 Meal Planning apps currently available on both iOS and Android:

1. Mealtime

The Mealtime app gives you the ability to create customizable Meal Plans in a user-friendly platform. These plans allow you to tailor your plans based on your diet and excluding foods you don't like.

LINK: http://bit.ly/mealimeapp

2. Paprika

The Paprika app is essentially a recipe manager at the first glance, but once you get in you realize that it does so much more including menu planning.

LINK: http://bit.ly/paprikamealapp

3. PlateJoy

Another great app to assist with creating customized Meal Plans is PlateJoy. The PlateJoy app offers you the ability to Meal Plan for your whole family based on your current dietary preferences and weight goals.

LINK: http://bit.ly/platejoyapp

4. Plan to Eat

The Plan to Eat app and website gives you a platform to organize your favorite recipes into personal Meal Plans.

LINK: http://bit.ly/plantoeatapp

5. Yummly

Yummly is another Meal Plan app that is available on both a mobile and online platform. The platform allows you to search and save popular recipes from across the internet to create a Meal Plan that is customized to your specific tastes.

LINK: http://bit.ly/yummyapprecipes

Chapter 4

Getting Started with Meal Prep

Meal Prep Equipment

The great thing about Meal Prep is that you don't need to go out and purchase a ton of fancy or expensive equipment to get started. Great food can come from anything in your kitchen as long as your kitchen already has the basics.

So, what are the basics?

- **A Proper Kitchen Knife**

Don't get crazy! You don't need to go out and buy an entire set of Chef grade knives (unless you want to). However, it is essential to have at least one sharp 8 to 10-inch Chef's knife. They are often inexpensive and save you time doing prep work while offering a safe environment. Believe it or not, a dull knife is far more dangerous in the kitchen than a sharp one!

- **A Decent Sized Cutting Board**

A cutting board goes hand in hand with a sharp knife. This will protect the finish on your cupboards and prevent you from chipping the edges of your knife or losing a finger attempting to cut something in your hand. Try to aim for an 18 x10x1.5 (or larger) wooden or polypropylene board. It's helpful to have separate boards for produce and meat.

- **12-Inch Non-stick Skillet**

A skillet is essentially a frying pan with a handle. Getting a 12 – inch pan is essential as it allows you to easily prepare multiple servings at once. Not all skillets are non-stick, so you want to take care when selecting your pan. This will aid in both ease of cooking and clean up.

- **Sheet Pan & Silicone Baking Mat**

This one is another self-explanatory piece of equipment. Baking and roasting make for a huge time saver in Meal Prepping as such you want to have a large baking sheet.

I recommend buying an 18x13-inch sheet pan so that you can cook multiple servings without overcrowding.

A silicone baking mat does the non-stick function for your baking sheet making it clean up faster.

- **Baking Dish (Preferably Glass or Ceramic)**

This ties in with having a baking sheet. A baking dish, however, gives you the means to create delicious casseroles, Mac N cheese, lasagna and so much more. Again, aim for the larger sizes. I recommend getting a set of 3: one 9x13-inch dish, one 8x11-inch dish, and one 9x9-inch dish.

- **Blender**

The quality of your blender can do wonders for your prep. I recommend getting a glass blender that can crush ice. This will give you the ability to create tasty smoothies, sauces, and dressings.

- **Heat-proof Spatula**

A spatula is a flat kitchen tool used to stir and scrape bowls and pans.

- **Mixing Bowls**

You want to have multiple bowls of different sizes on hand. Aim to get glass, ceramic, or stainless-steel bowls. Avoid plastic as often they get discolored easily and they soak in different food scents.

- **Measuring Cups & Spoons**

Try to get measuring cups and spoons for both wet and dry ingredients as they are measured differently. I would recommend trying to get standard sets of metal or plastic cups and spoons for your dry ingredients.

A standard set of dry measuring cups will include a: 1/3 cup, 1/4 cup, 1/2 cup, and 1 cup. Though there will be sets that include a 1/8 cup.

Liquid Measuring cups are typically made of either glass or plastic. I recommend getting 2 separate glass cups: one 2-cup and 4-cup liquid measuring cup. If you are only able to afford one, go with the 4-cup glass cup.

Measuring spoons typically come in both metal and plastic, either one works well. So, try to get a standard set in your preferred material. A standard set will include ¼, ½, and 1 teaspoon, and 1 tablespoon in terms of sizes.

It is fully possible to Meal Prep with only the basics; however, your journey will be a bit easier if you also have access to a:

- Kitchen Scale
- Slow Cooker
- Food Processor
- Paring Knife
- Citrus Zester
- Electronic or Outdoor Grill
- Muffin Tins

I won't go in detail about these items because I don't want you to feel the need to go out and buy them as they are in no way essential when first getting started. They are, however, good assets if you already have access to them.

Grocery Shopping Tips

There are a variety of things you must consider when creating your shopping list. Including but certainly not limited to your budget, dietary preferences as well as any food allergies or sensitivities that you may have.

Let's start by discussing a few tips you can employ to maintain a Mediterranean-friendly kitchen.

Tip #1: **Pick Products from the Frozen Aisle**

Frozen foods, such as fish or produce, tend to be great cost-effective staples for the Mediterranean kitchen.

Take vegetables, for example. They are generally frozen at the point where they are at their peak of freshness. This helps them to retain the most nutrients possible. What's even better is that they can be stored for multiple weeks, making it possible for you to fill your freezer with them so you can create healthy meals with what's already in your freezer.

Tip #2: Try to Avoid Storing Too Many Sweets in Your Kitchen

This may sound like a silly tip, but the reality is many people struggle with sticking to the Mediterranean Diet because they have sweets and other non-Mediterranean foods like red meat or sweets that should only be consumed occasionally readily on hand.

Why leave it up to your willpower to resist? Get rid of the unnecessary sweets from your kitchen instead try to stock up quality nuts or seeds that are rich in healthy fats and antioxidants.

Tip #3: Learn How to Spot High-quality Olive Oil

It is believed that Olive Oil is graded on its acidity level, taste, and processing method with Extra Virgin Olive Oil being the healthiest of the batch. EVO has the most flavor of the batch as it is extracted without any chemicals or heat leaving all its antioxidants and micronutrients intact.

Plain Olive oil and Light Olive oil are not bad, as they are made from refined olive oil. They contain a healthy fatty acid profile but often lack in the antioxidant department when compared to EVO. They also aren't as heat sensitive and tend to not retain all their nutrients.

Tip #4: Be Sure to Select the Right Alcohol

The Mediterranean Diet allows for one glass of red wine when medical conditions and lifestyles permit. So be sure to check your doctor if needed, and once you get the go-ahead, stock your kitchen with red wine.

Tip #5: Plan with Food Allergies & Intolerances in Mind

In most of these cases, you'll need to cut things from your recipes and make creative substitutions. Let's explore some of the common allergens and possible substitutions.

Dairy Products

If you or someone in your family are Lactose Intolerant or vegan you will probably want to remove dairy products like milk, cheese, and butter from your grocery list. Luckily, there are a bunch of substitute products available on the market such as nut and soy-based milk. In terms of cheeses, there has been a boom of plant-based cheeses on the market that are in fact tasty. The largest brands to date are Daiya, Follow Your Heart, Kite Hill, and Miyoko's.

Eggs

If you need to avoid eggs for medical or personal recipes you can substitute eggs in baking recipes using what's known as a flax egg. To create a flax egg simply combine 1 tablespoon of flaxseed meal with 2.5 tablespoons of water. Stir the mixture well then set to chill for about 15 minutes before using the mixture to replace 1 egg. This is also perfect for vegan recipes.

Nuts

Nut allergies in most cases are very serious. There are most cases you would want to simply avoid any recipe that uses nuts which includes the byproducts. In the event, however, that avoiding the recipe is not possible, consider substituting them with plant-based seeds like pumpkin seeds, sunflower seeds, or even soybeans.

Gluten

Celiac Disease is an auto-immune disease in which gluten damages your small intestines. People with this disease have to avoid products such as wheat, barley, and rye. This, unfortunately, includes most commercial flours and byproducts. However, you can get substitutes such as quinoa, millet, and certain plant-based options and gluten-free flours.

Be sure to check your product labels as they are generally clearly labeled as Gluten-Free.

The Best Food to Meal Prep

If you look back onto the Mediterranean Diet pyramid featured in the first chapter, you will realize that the majority of your meal will be made up of plant-based foods. So, expect to find a lot of whole grains, fruits, and vegetables. With few servings of seafood, poultry, and meat.

That does not mean, however, that omnivorous eaters cannot Meal Prep on the Mediterranean Diet. It does mean, however, that you will need to be mindful of your Meal Plan so as to be sure the main portion of each meal is something plant-based.

For this reason, it is vital that we understand the 'shelf life' of common staples so that you know what ingredients are safe to keep for longer periods.

So, what are the Mediterranean Staples?

The 13 Mediterranean Staples

Staple	Shelf Life
Extra – Virgin Olive Oil	About 20 months
	(Useful to store for long periods, but ultimately perishable)
Canned Fish	1 – 5 years
	(Can be stored for years without going bad)
Dried Fruit	6 months -1 year
	(Dependent on the temperature they are stored. At 60ºF they last up to a year and 6 months at 80ºF)

Raw or Roasted Nuts and Seeds	6 months -1 year
	(Typically, when stored in an airtight container and placed in a cool dark place)
Whole-Grain Staples	3 Days
	(Should be stored in a cool, dry place in an airtight container, once opened. Store in the refrigerator)
Tomatoes	3 days to 3 months
	(The stage and storage of the tomato play a huge role in its shelf life. 1 -5 days when green; stored in the pantry. 5 – 7 days once ripe, stored in the refrigerator. 2-3 months if stored in the freezer.)
Olives	3 days
	(Olives stored in its liquid lasts up to 2 weeks, while without its liquid lasts only 3 days)
Whole-Grain Crackers	About 6 – 9 months
	(When stored in an unopened package)
Canned Beans	2 – 5 years
	(When stored in a dry, cooled place)

Herbs and Spices	1 – 3 years
	(Dried and ground lasts for up to a year, whole keeps for 3 and salt lasts indefinitely)
Onions and Garlic	3 months
	(They tend to go soft and grow blemishes after 3 months)
Plain Greek Yogurt	14 – 24 days
	(When sealed well and refrigerated)
Artisanal Cheeses	4 – 8 months
	(4 months in the refrigerator and 8 in the freezer)

10 Steps to Successful Meal Prep

Step 1: Decide on what your favorite ingredients are and determine how to spin them into complete meals.

Step 2: Create a monthly spreadsheet or calendar so that you can record all your grocery shopping lists, favorite recipe websites, and all your meal ideas so that you can easily access them.

Step 3: Create a Meal Prep schedule. Decide what day of the week you will go plan your meals for the upcoming week, create your lists, grocery shop, and prepare your meals.

Step 4: Start a collection of healthy recipes. Get creative, consider adding in magazine clips, newspaper sheets, or even copies of your favorite recipes from the internet and recipe books so that when you are ready to create your Meal Plan you can easily draw from your collection.

Step 5: Take a breather and have fun with it! Create different themes for the days of the week. You can create Movie Mondays with meals you would typically enjoy on a movie night, Taco Tuesdays, or make up your own like Wacky Wednesday or whatever you want. It's important that you try to keep your Meal Planning fun so that you don't divert from it. The more creativity you incorporate the better it will be.

Step 6: Create your shopping lists! Don't go crazy when you are just starting out! Instead, try to start small, if you are a complete beginner consider starting with planning for just 3 days a week and get comfortable with that then you can move on as you get more comfortable.

Step 7: Go shopping! Take the list you created and head to the store. Stick to your list, do not go pursuing the dessert isles if there is no dessert on your list. Home in and stick to the stuff you need for the week.

Step 8: Stop and picture your portions. Now take a look at your cart and your list. If you have to question if you have enough food, you may have skipped something on your list. Be sure you have everything and head home to prep your ingredients.

Step 9: <u>Prep your ingredients and label everything before you begin cooking</u>. Having everything prepped ahead of time will drastically cut the time taken to prep all your meals.

Step 10: <u>Prepare, portion & safely store your meals.</u> You have completed all your planning, your ingredients are purchased, and you've done your prep work. It's finally time to prepare your meals. Try to group all the like takes together. For example, if you have two recipes that will need to use the oven, aim to prepare them at the same time, or at least close together if they use separate temperatures. This will help you to multitask and get through all your cooking efficiently. Clean as you go, then portion and label all your meals before storing.

Chapter 5

Mix & Match Healthy Meals

How to Mix and Match Healthy Meals

Alright so now that you understand a bit more about the basics of the Med Diet and what Meal Prep is, let's take a deeper look at how to formulate an actual plan; specifically how to mix and match healthy meals in a smart way. The main thing you want to understand is how to decide what ingredients or meals will last for more than a couple of days while still tasting good.

Below we will deep dive into the four major food groups and tips for the ingredients that will last you through a week of Meal Prep.

Let's begin with your proteins!

1. Eggs

Eggs can be prepared in several ways in Meal Prep to last you through the week.

Here are 3 of my favorite Meal Prepping egg methods:

Good ole Hard-boil

Simply boil, portion them in their shell, and store. Once you are ready use them that's when you peel them. These can last you the whole week using this method.

Create a Frittata or Egg Muffins

A frittata makes for an easy meal for any time of day. Preparing your seasoned egg mixture in a muffin tin gives you delicious egg muffins that make for a delicious portable breakfast. Ensure that your frittata or egg muffins are fully cooled and properly covered before refrigerating. This prep will be good for about 4 days.

Devil Eyes

Mash and combine your yolks with your favorite ingredients to create delicious deviled eggs. This preparation won't last as long but if stored separately in a covered container can be used for the first 2 or 3 days of your prep.

2. Beans & Edible Seeds

Beans and other edible seeds, such as lentils, chickpeas, kidney beans, dry peas, and pinto beans, to name a few are great sources of protein for vegetarians and omnivores alike. They are also perfect for Meal Prep when keeping the following tips in mind:

Soak Your Pulses

Pulses are generally sold dried which makes them great for storage but terrible for cooking quickly. As such consider soaking your harder pulses such as kidney peas, chickpeas, etc. overnight to help them cook faster.

Soaking can also give them a creamier texture once cooked. Split Peas and lentils naturally cook quickly hence don't need soaking; in fact, they may lose their shape if soaked. Store your pulses in their liquid until you are ready to cook them.

Cooked pulses will remain fresh for about 3 days in the refrigerator. If frozen, they can last for a good 2 months. Be careful though so keeping them frozen for too long can ruin the flavor.

3. Chicken

Chicken is a very versatile source of protein. It can be baked, grilled, stewed, and even poached. You can use your prepared chicken to create salads, sandwiches, grain bowls, and even pasta.

Once cooked, your chicken will last about 4 days in the fridge. Anything you plan on using after then prep and store in individual freezer bags until it's time for serving.

Now let's explore common Mediterranean grains!

4. Brown rice

Whole wheat grains play a large part in your Mediterranean diet prep as they are more nutritious than their white, processed counterpart. Brown rice can be used as a foundation for jambalaya, veggie burgers, and fried rice.

Brown rice once cooked should be cooled on a sheet pan and stored in the refrigerator in airtight containers. It will last for about 4 to 6 days.

5. Quinoa

Quinoa is a powerhouse throughout many cuisines and is super useful in Meal Prep as it is packed with nutrients. Soak your quinoa for at least 2 hours before cooking to make cooking easier. Cooked quinoa when stored in an airtight container will remain fresh for 5 days to a week in the refrigerator. In the freezer, it will last for at least a month.

6. Oatmeal

Oatmeal can be cooked and stored in individual containers in the fridge or freezer for 4 to 6 days. You can prep and store your toppings such as chia seeds or berries until it's time to serve.

7. Pasta

Whole wheat pasta is inexpensive, delicious and can be prepped for the whole week if stored properly. Once cooked, store in an airtight container without the sauce and toppings then assemble when it's time to serve. Cooked pasta will last for up to 5 days in the fridge or 2 - 3 months in the freezer.

What About Fruits?

8. Fruits

Fruits can be enjoyed cooked, fresh, or frozen in your Meal Prep and the life span of each will of course vary. Cooked fruits tend to go mushy quicker due to the broken-down fiber as such they should be used within the first 2 days of your prep and must be refrigerated or frozen. Fresh whole fruits can easily last up to a week while frozen fruits will keep for 2 – 3 months. Once the fruits are peeled or cut, they will keep for up to 3 days in a chilled airtight container.

Does the same apply to vegetables?

9. Vegetables

There are a ton of vegetables to choose from when Meal Prepping on the Mediterranean diet. When stored fresh they will last in the refrigerator for 5-7 days. Salads should be stored without dressing and dressed when ready to serve.

Cooked vegetables can last for up to 4 days in the refrigerator and 1 – 3 months in the freezer.

Master Your Portions

Learning how to master portions while Meal Prepping can be great for maintaining or losing weight. The right portions will ensure you remain on target with your desired calorie count and aid in weight loss if that's your goal.

The recommended portions on the Mediterranean Diet are as follows:

○ **Breakfast**

Your breakfast plate (2 cup serving) should look like this:

- ½ cup Fruits
- 1 Cup Juices/Soy Milk
- 1 Cup Whole Grain
- ½ oz. Nuts & Seeds

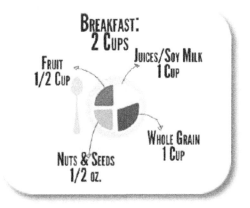

○ **Lunch**

Your lunch plate should look like this:

- ¼ of your plate should be lean or plant-based protein (about 4 ounces), eggs, lentils, or beans

- Another ¼ (about ¾ - 1 cup) should consist of whole grains

- And a 1/2 of your plate (about 1 cup) filled with fruit or vegetables

○ **Dinner**

Your dinner plate should look like this:

- 1 serving lean or plant-based protein, eggs, lentils, or beans

- 2 servings whole grains

- 4 servings with fruit or vegetables

- 1 – 2 servings Nuts and Seeds

- 6 - 8 Glasses of water

- 1 Glass of Red Wine

- 1 Serving Healthy Oil

- 2 Servings Low or Non-Fat Dairy

Understanding The Essential Macros

Everything we eat is categorized into a variety of smaller groups known as macronutrients, or macros for short. The three main macros are fats, proteins, and carbohydrates. Unlike the other restrictive diets, the Mediterranean Diet is more a style of eating.

If you are concerned about maintaining a certain ratio of macros due to dietary restrictions, then you should use a reputable macro calculator app such as **MyMacros**, **LoseIt**, or **Lifesum**. They will ask you to enter general information used for weight management such as your age, gender, weight, height, activity level, body fat percentage, and to determine whether your goal is to lose weight or to simply maintain.

The calculator will then work out all the information you need regarding your calorie intake and the breakdown of macronutrients. The calculator will provide you with the exact number of fats, carbs, and proteins you should be eating a day, in grams.

Once you have calculated your needs, you will have a clear idea of how to plan your meals going forward. It's a great idea to download an app such as **MyPlate** or **MyFitnessPal**, log in your macro goals, then add in all your foods to make sure they fit the correct requirements. It does take a few days to get the hang of it, but it becomes second nature quickly!

Let's look at some of the macronutrients:

Carbs

Carbohydrates are most recognized as "starchy" foods such as bread, pasta, potatoes, and rice. However, carbohydrates include sugars and sugar-containing foods such as fruit, candy, cakes, alcohol, and other similar foods. When you eat carbs, your body turns them into glucose (blood sugar), which is then used for energy. As soon as the amount of sugar in the blood is raised, your pancreas gets the message to pump out more insulin, so the blood sugar can be processed and moved around the body as energy. The recommended percentage of carbohydrates is 45 to 65 percent of your total daily calories.

Protein

Protein can be converted to glucose if too much of it is consumed. It is recommended that you consume only moderate portions of protein as too much will cause your body to store excess glucose. This will, in turn, become stored fat. Your muscles and tissues need protein to grow and repair so moderate portions are still required. The recommended daily intake is 0.8 grams of protein per kilogram of body weight or 0.36 grams per pound.

Fat

Fat can be broken down into 3 categories: Polyunsaturated, Saturated, and Monounsaturated fats. I won't confuse you with the science behind the three of them, but I will provide you with this tip. Fats which are "whole" or "from the source" such as eggs, grass-fed meats, heavy cream, butter, fresh fatty fish such as salmon are all healthy sources of fat.

Products that have been processed and refined down to a "different" form than how they started are "bad" fats, such as margarine and vegetable oils (apart from olive oil). If you are unsure if a fatty food is okay or not, just think: is this in a packet with lots of ingredients and scientific words? Has it been processed to the extent where it comes in a different form from where it started? If so, then avoid it. If you can say, "this food hasn't been processed, it is reasonably close to its original form, and the ingredients list is very short," then go ahead and add it to your list. In all cases, the dietary reference intake for fat in adults is 20% to 35% of daily total calories from fat.

Customizing Your Meal Plan

Have you ever tried to lose weight by cutting down on food? Do you feel hungry after eating less food than you normally do? Does it make you angry not being satisfied with the amount of food you eat?

There are other ways of weighing less that are a more steady and slow approach towards aiming for weight loss. You can do this by cutting down calories in your diet, taking a nutritional diet, and performing good physical activity. With this kind of diet plan, you will not only be satisfied, but you will also be healthy.

People lose weight by cutting down on the number of calories, not by cutting the serving of the food. You could do this by lowering the calorie intake and eat foods that have fewer calories and increase fiber foods in your diet. Foods that are rich in fiber content are not only healthy, but they will contribute greatly towards weight loss.

The average calorie intake that a person should take is 1200 calories per day. An example is a plate of mac and cheese. By the looks and sound of it, we feel that it is a super cheesy meal and it has 540 calories in one plate that serves one.

You could remake this plate and serve it with fewer calories and still, it will taste delicious. For example, you could alter the milk by using nonfat milk and you can also use light cream cheese instead of full-fat cheddar cheese. Instead of margarine, use butter. Add vegetables such as carrots or broccoli to make it more nutritious.

PART 3: FOUR WEEKS MEAL PLAN

Chapter 6

Week One

Alright, we are finally at the home stretch! It's time to get cooking! This 4-week Meal Plan will include 24 amazing recipes (6 per week) to get you into the swing of things.

Each week will include universal breakfast options, as well as a vegetarian and omnivorous option for lunch and dinner. The servings and amounts featured are for 1 person so you will need to multiply the quantities in the ingredients and shopping lists by the specific number of people you are prepping for.

Meal Plan

	Breakfast	Lunch	Dinner
Day 1	Oatmeal with Fruits & Nuts	Roasted Beet Salad with Ricotta Cheese	Chicken Paillard with Grilled Vegetables

Day 2	Oatmeal with Fruits & Nuts	Grilled Spiced Turkey Burger	Baked Chicken with Brown Rice & Veggies
Day 3	Oatmeal with Fruits & Nuts	Roasted Beet Salad with Ricotta Cheese	Chicken Paillard with Grilled Vegetables
Day 4	Oatmeal with Fruits & Nuts	Grilled Spiced Turkey Burger	Baked Chicken with Brown Rice & Veggies
Day 5	Oatmeal with Fruits & Nuts	Roasted Beet Salad with Ricotta Cheese	Chicken Paillard with Grilled Vegetables
Day 6	Mediterranean Omelet with Wheat Bread & Blueberries	Grilled Spiced Turkey Burger	Baked Chicken with Brown Rice & Veggies
Day 7	Mediterranean Omelet with Wheat Bread & Blueberries	Roasted Beet Salad with Ricotta Cheese	Chicken Paillard with Grilled Vegetables

Shopping List

PANTRY (Check your pantry before shopping as you may already have some of these items)

- Salt (1 Box, If Needed)

- Pepper (1 Box, If Needed)

- White Pepper (1/8 Tsp.)
- Cinnamon (¼ Tsp.)
- Mustard Vinaigrette (4.4g)
- Curry Powder (1 Tbsp)
- Whole Wheat Flour (4 Oz)
- Paprika (1/4 Tsp)

FRESH PRODUCE

- Yellow Onion (2 Medium)
- Garlic (1 Peg)
- Spinach (2 cups)
- Roma Tomato (3)
- Kalamata Olives (8 Pieces)
- Fresh Parsley (1.5 bunch)
- Peach (1)
- Red Beets (8.8 Oz, Large)
- Yellow Beets (8.8 Oz, Small)
- Mesclun (4.3 Oz.)
- Cilantro (1 Bunch)

- Fresh Rosemary (1 Tbsp)
- Grilled Vegetable Medley (1 Pack)
- Fresh Rosemary (12 Sprigs)
- Lemon (1)
- Blueberries (0.3 oz)
- Broccoli (3 oz, florets)

PROTEIN

- Eggs (4, large)
- Turkey (14.4 oz, ground)
- Chicken breast (4 (24 oz), boneless, skinless)
- Fryer chicken parts (120 oz.)

DAIRY

- Skim milk (3L)
- feta cheese (15 tbsp, crumbled)
- Ricotta cheese (2.1 oz)

GRAINS, NUTS, SEEDS, AND LEGUMES (Check your pantry before shopping as you may already have some of these items)

- Oats (2 ½ cup, raw)
- Assorted nuts, blanched and slivered (0.3 oz)
- Walnuts (0.1 oz)
- Whole Wheat Bread (1 loaf)
- Brown Rice (1 cup)

DRIED/DEHYDRATED FRUITS & VEGETABLES

- Peach (1, chopped)
- Raisins (2 cups)
- Dried cranberries (2½ cup)

HERBS (Check your pantry before shopping as you may already have some of these items)

- Dried thyme (1 container, if needed -1/8 tsp needed for recipe)
- Coriander (1/2 tsp, ground)
- Cumin (1/4 tsp, ground)
- Cardamom (1/4 tsp, ground)

OTHER (Check your pantry before shopping as you may already have some of these items)

- Extra Virgin Olive Oil (16.5 fl oz)
- Honey (2 ½ tsp., optional)
- Tomato Raisin Chutney (1 small bottle)
- Lemon Juice (3 fl oz)

EQUIPMENT

- Chef's knife
- Cutting board
- Measuring cups and spoons

- Mixing bowls
- Spatulas
- Zester/Small grater
- Kitchen Tongs (If using a grill)
- 2 (18x13-inch) sheet pans
- Silicone baking mats or parchment paper
- 12-inch skillet

- 8x2-inch baking dish
- (if using the oven to broil)

Step by Step Prep

1. Flatten your chicken for your Chicken Paillard with Grilled Vegetables and set to marinate at least 2 hours before you begin your remaining prep.

2. Set your oven to preheat to 400 degrees F.

3. While your oven is preheating, proceed to chop all ingredients to match the recipe ingredient lists.

4. Combine your flour and seasoning for Baked Chicken with Brown Rice & Veggies.

5. Wash, dry, season, and coat your chicken pieces for your Baked Chicken and place them on a lined baking sheet. Toss in your broccoli around your chicken.

6. Set your beets for Roasted Beet Salad with Ricotta Cheese and chicken for Baked Chicken with Brown Rice & Veggies in the preheated oven to bake.

7. Set your brown rice on to cook for your Baked Chicken with Brown Rice & Veggies

8. Cook your onions for your Grilled Spiced Turkey Burger then set aside to cool completely.

9. Cook your Mediterranean Omelet with Wheat Bread & Blueberries. Portion into 2 plates and set aside to cool before refrigerating or freezing. Store your bread at room temperature and your blueberries separately in the fridge.

10. At 45 minutes test the temperature of your Baked Chicken with Brown Rice & Veggies. If down set aside to cool.

11. Form burger patties for your Grilled Spiced Turkey Burger place on your baking sheet and set aside until beets are done.

12. Once your beets are cooked, remove from the oven, and set aside to cool.

13. Switch your oven to broil and allow it to preheat to high (at least 450 F).

14. Clean up the tools and counters.

15. Portion your chicken and rice for your Baked Chicken with Brown Rice & Veggies and store your Veggies in a separate container.

16. Portion your veggies and dressing separately for your Chicken Paillard with Grilled Vegetables and refrigerate.

17. Set your Grilled Spiced Turkey Burger, plus your chicken and vegetables from your Chicken Paillard with Grilled Vegetables recipes, and set under your broiler to cook.

18. Trim, peel, and cut your beets for the Roasted Beet Salad with Ricotta Cheese. Portion your beets with the vegetables and store separately from your dressing, ricotta, and walnuts.

19. Make the Oatmeal with Fruits & Nuts, spoon into 5 containers, and refrigerate.

Chapter 7

Week Two

Meal Plan

	Breakfast	Lunch	Dinner
Day 1	Breakfast Couscous	Tomato Tea Party Sandwiches	Mediterranean Sushi
Day 2	Breakfast Couscous	Veggie Shish Kebabs	Pan- Smoked Trout Fillet with Pepper Salad
Day 3	Breakfast Couscous	Tomato Tea Party Sandwiches	Mediterranean Sushi
Day 4	Breakfast Couscous	Veggie Shish Kebabs	Pan- Smoked Trout Fillet with Pepper Salad
Day 5	Breakfast Couscous	Tomato Tea Party Sandwiches	Mediterranean Sushi
Day 6	Greek Yogurt Bowl	Veggie Shish Kebabs	Pan- Smoked Trout Fillet with Pepper Salad

| Day 7 | Greek Yogurt Bowl | Tomato Tea Party Sandwiches | Mediterranean Sushi |

Shopping List

PANTRY (Check your pantry before shopping as you may already have some of these items)

- Black Pepper
- Salt
- 2" Cinnamon Stick (3)

FRESH PRODUCE

- Garlic (2 cloves)
- Cucumber (12 large)
- Tomato (1 large)
- Cherry tomatoes (9)
- Raspberry (1 cup)
- Strawberries (6, hulled and sliced)
- Blueberries (1 cup, fresh)
- Zucchini (3, medium)

PROTEIN

- Trout fillet (12 oz)

DAIRY

- Feta Cheese (3 Tbsp., Low-Fat, Crumbled)
- Mozzarella Balls (9 Low-Fat)
- Skim Milk (9 Cups)
- Greek Yogurt (2 Cups, Plain)
- Ricotta cheese (4 oz)

GRAINS, NUTS, SEEDS, AND LEGUMES (Check your pantry before shopping as you may already have some of these items)

- Whole Wheat Bread (10 Slices)
- Whole Wheat Couscous (3 Cups, Uncooked)

DRIED/DEHYDRATED FRUITS & VEGETABLES

- Raisins and Currants (3/4 Cup)
- Dried Apricots (1 ½ Cup)
- Sun-dried Tomatoes (3 tbsp.)

HERBS (Check your pantry before shopping as you may already have some of these items)

- Ground Coriander (1/4 Tsp)
- Ground Cumin (1/4 Tsp)
- Ground Cloves (1/8 Tsp)
- Ground Fennel (1/4 Tsp)
- Basil Leaves (16)

OTHER (Check your pantry before shopping as you may already have some of these items)

- Roasted Pepper Salad (12 Oz.)

- Extra Virgin Olive Oil (4.44 Fl Oz)
- Hummus (3 Tbsp.)
- Honey (10 Tbsp)

EQUIPMENT

- Chef's knife
- Cutting board
- Measuring cups and spoons
- Mixing bowls
- Wooden Skewers (9)
- Spatulas
- Zester/Small grater
- Kitchen Tongs (If using a grill)
- 2 (18x13-inch) sheet pans
- Silicone baking mats or parchment paper
- 12-inch skillet
- 8x2-inch baking dish
- (if using the oven to broil)
- Wood chips
- Dutch Oven/Large pot

- Wire rack/Oven rack
- Vegetable sheer

Step by Step Prep

1. Set up your stovetop smoker as directed in the Pan-Smoked Trout Fillet with Pepper Salad recipe and set your oven to preheat to 400 degrees F.

2. While your oven is preheating, proceed to chop all ingredients to match the recipe ingredient lists.

3. Prepare season and coat trout for Pan- Smoked Trout Fillet with Pepper Salad with oil. Lay the trout fillets on the rack, cover, and turn the heat to medium-low. Transfer your fillet to the preheated oven.

4. Clean up the tools and counters.

5. Create and portion your Breakfast Couscous recipe in the refrigerator when cool.

6. Make the Greek Yogurt Bowl, spoon into 2 containers, and refrigerate without toppings. Add honey and toppings when it's time to serve.

7. Remove your fish from the oven and set to cool. Portion and refrigerate once cool.

8. Portion pepper salad for Pan- Smoked Trout Fillet with Pepper Salad and refrigerate. Add it to trout when ready to serve.

9. Portion ingredients for Tomato Tea Party Sandwiches and store separately. Toast bread on the day you will be serving and assemble when ready to serve.

10. Create and portion your Veggie Shish Kebabs. Refrigerate then add bread when ready to serve.

11. Create and portion your Mediterranean Sushi. Refrigerate.

Chapter 8

Week Three

Meal Plan

	Breakfast	**Lunch**	**Dinner**
Day 1	Buckwheat Pancakes	Baked Fish with Tomatoes and Mushrooms	Tomato Basil Stuffed Peppers
Day 2	Buckwheat Pancakes	Crispy Falafel	Chunky Vegetable Soup
Day 3	Italian Omelet	Baked Fish with Tomatoes and Mushrooms	Tomato Basil Stuffed Peppers
Day 4	Italian Omelet	Crispy Falafel	Chunky Vegetable Soup
Day 5	Italian Omelet	Baked Fish with Tomatoes and Mushrooms	Tomato Basil Stuffed Peppers

| Day 6 | Italian Omelet | Crispy Falafel | Chunky Vegetable Soup |
| Day 7 | Italian Omelet | Baked Fish with Tomatoes and Mushrooms | Tomato Basil Stuffed Peppers |

Shopping List

PANTRY (Check your pantry before shopping as you may already have some of these items)

- Stevia Sweetener (2½ Tsp)
- Vanilla Extract (1/2 Tsp)
- Salt
- Pepper
- Baking Soda (1/2 Tsp)
- Baking Powder (3 Tsp)
- Cumin (½ Tbsp.)
- Cayenne (½ Tsp.)
- Italian Seasoning

FRESH PRODUCE

- Tomato (5 Medium)
- Garlic (12 cloves)
- Mushrooms (6 Cup, Sliced)
- Zucchini (5 Cup, Sliced)
- Onion (3)
- Shallots (1 Oz)
- Bell Peppers (4, Color of Your Preference)
- Carrots (4)
- Butternut Squash (4)
- Celery Stalks (4)

PROTEIN

- Fish (4, Whole and Small, 12 Oz Each)
- Eggs (22)
- Chickpeas (1 Cup)
- Tofu (16 Oz., Crumbled)
- Kidney Beans (4 Cans, Drained and Rinsed)

DAIRY

- Buttermilk (2½ Cup)
- Mozzarella (2 ½ Cup)
- Feta Cheese (¾ Cup)
- Heavy Cream (1/3 Cup)

GRAINS, NUTS, SEEDS, AND LEGUMES (Check your pantry before shopping as you may already have some of these items)

- Buckwheat Flour (2 Cups)
- Brown Rice (1 ½ Cups, Cooked)

HERBS (Check your pantry before shopping as you may already have some of these items)

- Basil (4¾ Tsp, Dried)
- Thyme (1/2 Tsp. Dried)
- Coriander (½ Tbsp.)
- Parsley (2 Cups, Dried)
- Cilantro (1/3 Cup)
- Dill (¼ Cup)
- Oregano (2 Tsp)
- Bay Leaves (7)

OTHER (Check your pantry before shopping as you may already have some of these items)

- Clarified Ghee (2 Tbsp)
- Extra Virgin Olive Oil (36¼ Tbsp)
- Tomato Concasse (6.4 Oz)
- Dry White Wine (3.2 Fl Oz)
- Sesame Seeds (1 Tbsp., Toasted)
- Tomato Sauce (1 Can)

- Tomatoes (2¾ Cups Canned)
- Vegetable Broth (7.2 Cups)
- Spatulas
- Zester/Small grater
- Kitchen Tongs (If using a grill)
- 2 (18x13-inch) sheet pans

EQUIPMENT

- Chef's knife
- Cutting board
- Measuring cups and spoons
- Mixing bowls
- Wooden Skewers (9)
- Silicone baking mats or parchment paper
- 12-inch skillet
- 8x2-inch baking dish
- (if using the oven to broil)

Step by Step Prep

1. Chop all ingredients to match the recipe ingredient lists.

2. Cook the vegetables and tofu as directed in the Baked Fish with Tomatoes and Mushrooms and Tomato Basil Stuffed Peppers recipes.

3. Transfer the vegetables for the Baked Fish with Tomatoes and Mushroom to the bottom of your baking dish and set aside.

4. Scale, clean, and season the fish for your Baked Fish with Tomatoes and Mushroom recipe and set aside in a baking dish. Add in your remaining ingredients and set aside until the oven preheats.

5. Prepare the basil brown rice filling for your Tomato Basil Stuffed Peppers. Assemble your peppers and place them on a baking sheet. Set aside until the oven preheats.

6. Set your oven to preheat to 400 degrees F.

7. Clean up the tools and counters.

8. Form your Crispy Falafels and set to get firm.

9. Add your Baked Fish with Tomatoes and Mushrooms and Tomato Basil Stuffed Peppers into the preheated oven.

10. Create your Buckwheat Pancakes batter while the oven preheats and leave to rest.

11. Set the ingredients for your Chunky Vegetable Soup on to simmer.

12. Create your Buckwheat Pancakes. Portion and store once cool. Add your maple syrup or topping when ready to serve.

13. Switch off your soup. Portion and set to cool before refrigerating.

14. Create your Italian Omelet. Portion and store once cool.

15. Set your Baked Fish with Tomatoes and Mushrooms and Tomato Basil Stuffed Peppers to cool.

16. Fry your Crispy Falafels, then set to cool.

17. Portion your Baked Fish with Tomatoes and Mushrooms and Tomato Basil Stuffed Peppers and refrigerate.

18. Portion your cooled Crispy Falafels, and refrigerate.

Chapter 9

Week Four

Meal Plan

	Breakfast	Lunch	Dinner
Day 1	Kickstart Your Day Berry Smoothie	Onion Fried Eggs	Cheesy Eggplant Sandwiches
Day 2	Kickstart Your Day Berry Smoothie	Goat Cheese and Walnut Salad	Pan-Smoked Spiced Chicken Breasts with Fruit Salsa
Day 3	Simple Mediterranean Breakfast with Sashimi & Pickles	Onion Fried Eggs	Cheesy Eggplant Sandwiches
Day 4	Simple Mediterranean Breakfast with Sashimi & Pickles	Goat Cheese and Walnut Salad	Pan-Smoked Spiced Chicken Breasts with Fruit Salsa
Day 5	Simple Mediterranean Breakfast with Sashimi & Pickles	Onion Fried Eggs	Cheesy Eggplant Sandwiches

Day 6	Simple Mediterranean Breakfast with Sashimi & Pickles	Goat Cheese and Walnut Salad	Pan-Smoked Spiced Chicken Breasts with Fruit Salsa
Day 7	Simple Mediterranean Breakfast with Sashimi & Pickles	Onion Fried Eggs	Cheesy Eggplant Sandwiches

Shopping List

PANTRY (Check your pantry before shopping as you may already have some of these items)

- Sea Salt
- Black Pepper
- Breadcrumbs (1/4 Cup, Dry)
- Paprika (1/2 Tbsp)

FRESH PRODUCE

- Banana (2 Small, Peeled)
- Strawberries (3 ¼ Cup)
- Orange (2)

- Roma Tomatoes (5)
- Romaine Lettuce (9 Oz)
- Belgian Endive or Radicchio (2 Oz)
- Arugula (3 Oz)
- Bibb Lettuce (2 Oz)
- Onion (2 Large, Sliced)
- Garlic Clove (2, Minced)
- White Mushroom (1 cup)
- Wheatberries (9.75 Oz, With Pecans and Poblanos)
- Baby Spinach (2 Cups)

- Eggplant (3 Medium-Sized, Diced)

PROTEIN

- Eggs (21)
- Chicken breasts (3, boneless and skinless, 5 oz each)

DAIRY

- Greek Yogurt (1 Cup)
- Ricotta Cheese (1 Cup, Fresh)
- Fresh Goat's Milk Cheese (6.35 Oz, Preferably in Log Shape)
- Feta Cheese (4 Oz, Crumbled)
- Mozzarella Cheese (2/3 Cup, Low-Fat and Grated)
- Parmesan Cheese (4 Tbsp., Grated)

GRAINS, NUTS, SEEDS, AND LEGUMES (Check your pantry before shopping as you may already have some of these items)

- Flaxseeds (1.5 Tsp)
- Sourdough Rye Bread (5 Slice)
- Walnut Pieces (1.1 Oz)
- Whole Wheat Italian Bread (8 Pieces)

DRIED/DEHYDRATED FRUITS & VEGETABLES

- Sun-dried Tomatoes (2½ Cup, Chopped)

HERBS (Check your pantry before shopping as you may already have some of these items)

- Dried Thyme (1/2 Tbsp)
- Dried Basil (4¼ Tbsp)
- Cilantro Sprigs (1 Bunch, If Using)
- Ground Cumin (½ Tsp)
- Ground Coriander (½ Tsp)

OTHER ((Check your pantry before shopping as you may already have some of these items)

- Olive Oil (10 Tbsp)
- Red Wine Vinaigrette
- Fruit Salsa (6 Oz)

EQUIPMENT

- Chef's knife
- Cutting board
- Measuring cups and spoons
- Mixing bowls
- Wooden Skewers (9)
- Spatulas
- Zester/Small grater
- Kitchen Tongs (If using a grill)
- 2 (18x13-inch) sheet pans
- Silicone baking mats or parchment paper
- 12-inch skillet
- 8x2-inch baking dish
- (if using the oven to broil)

Step by Step Prep

1. Set up your stovetop smoker as directed in the Pan-Smoked Spiced Chicken Breasts with Fruit Salsa recipe and set your oven to preheat to 400 degrees F.

2. While your oven is preheating, proceed to chop all ingredients to match the recipe ingredient lists.

3. Prep, season and smoke your chicken based on instructions in the Pan-Smoked Spiced Chicken Breasts with Fruit Salsa.

4. Set your grill to preheat to high.

5. Transfer your Pan-Smoked Spiced Chicken Breasts with Fruit Salsa to your baking tray and transfer to the preheated oven.

6. Boil the eggs for your Simple Mediterranean Breakfast With Sashimi & Pickles and slice your salmon. Set your eggs to cool when cooked.

7. Prepare the eggplant and other veggies for the Cheesy Eggplant Sandwiches. Set your eggplant to grill then set to cool.

8. Create your Onion Fried Eggs, then set to cool.

9. Portion your ricotta, pickles, and olives for your Simple Mediterranean Breakfast With Sashimi & Pickles. Store all your components separately. Store eggs in shells. Remove your shells, then assemble ricotta and bread when ready to serve.

10. Portion and store all your ingredients for the Goat Cheese and Walnut Salad. Melt and toast the ingredients when ready to serve.

11. Set your Pan-Smoked Spiced Chicken Breasts with Fruit Salsa to cool.

12. Portion your Onion Fried Eggs, and refrigerate.

13. Make your Kickstart Your Day Berry Smoothie, portion, and refrigerate.

14. Portion and store your chicken for the Pan-Smoked Spiced Chicken Breasts with Fruit Salsa. Store the fruit salsa separately and add when ready to serve.

Chapter 10

Meal Plan Recipes

Breakfast

Kickstart Your Day Berry Smoothie

2

15 mins

0 mins

Allergy Warnings

Classification

Ingredients

Orange (2)

Greek yogurt (1 cup)

Banana (2 small, peeled)

Strawberries (3 ¼ cups)

Flaxseeds (1.5 tsp)

Directions

1. Cut the orange in half and remove the pit. Cube the pulp.

2. Place the ingredients in a food processor. Process until the ingredients are combined.

3. Serve immediately, or chill for an hour before serving.

Calories: 263 Fat: 2.9g Carbs: 49.6g Protein: 15.3g Fiber: 7.7g

Buckwheat Pancakes

2   20 mins   10 mins

Allergy Warnings   **Classification**

Ingredients

Egg (2)

Baking soda (1/2 tsp)

Baking powder (2 tsp)

Buttermilk (2½ cups)

Buckwheat flour (2 cups)

Stevia sweetener (2½ tsp)

Vanilla extract (1/2 tsp)

Salt (pinch)

Clarified ghee (2 tbsp)

Directions

1. Mix in a bowl, buckwheat flour, baking powder, soda, salt, and sweetener.

2. In a separate bowl, add all wet ingredients and whisk together.

3. Combine dry and wet ingredients to form a thick, smooth batter. Let it rest for 15 minutes.

4. Heat a skillet and add some olive oil.

5. In the center of the skillet, pour a large spoonful of batter a few inches in diameter and less than an inch in thickness.

6. When the batter starts bubbling over. This indicates it is time to flip it.

7. Flip the pancake and cook on both sides, pouring some more olive oil if needed to prevent sticking.

8. Pancake is done once it is brown, in about 2-3 minutes. Repeat these steps for the remaining batter.

9. Serve the pancakes warm with maple syrup, fruit, or honey.

Calories: 626 Fat: 10.7g Carbs: 109.8g Protein: 30.8g Fiber: 12g

Breakfast Couscous

5

20 mins

15 mins

Allergy Warnings

Classification

Ingredients

Whole-wheat couscous (3 cups, uncooked)

Skim milk (9 cups)

2" cinnamon stick (3)

Honey (6 tbsp)

Pinch of salt

Olive oil (4 tbsp, divided)

Raisins and currants (3/4 cup)

Dried apricots (1 ½ cups)

Directions

1. In a medium pan, combine cinnamon and milk and let boil for 3 minutes, stirring constantly.

2. Remove from heat; add the couscous, dried fruits, currants and salt, and 4 tsp of honey to the pan. Mix well.

3. Cover and set aside for 15 minutes.

4. Pour into 4 serving bowls and add 1 tsp olive oil and ½ tsp honey on top of each bowl. Stir and serve immediately.

Calories: 426 Fat: 11g Carbs: 62g Protein: 21g Fiber: 4g

Oatmeal with Fruit & Nuts

　5　　　　　15 mins　　　15 mins

Allergy Warnings　　　　　**Classification**

Ingredients

Oats (2 ½ cup, raw)

Skim milk or water (5 cups)

Cinnamon (1 ¼ tsp)

Peach (1, chopped)

Handful of raisins

Dried cranberries (1 ¼ cup)

Assorted nuts, blanched and slivered to sprinkle on top

Honey (2 ½ tsp., optional)

Directions

1. Cook the oats as per instructions and then add the remaining ingredients.

2. Add seasonal fruits and nuts to enhance the flavor of the oatmeal.

3. Add blueberries, strawberries, and maple syrup for a more classic combination. Enjoy!

Calories: 211 Fat: 1g Carbs: 40g Protein: 10g Fiber: 3.3g

Greek Yogurt Bowl

2

15 mins

0 mins

Allergy Warnings   **Classification**

Ingredients

Greek yogurt (2 cups, plain)

Raspberries (1 cup)

Strawberries (6, hulled and sliced)

Blueberries (1 cup, fresh)

Organic honey (4 tbsp, raw)

Directions

1. Place Greek yogurt in a bowl. Add the sliced banana and berries.

2. Drizzle honey on top. Top with seeds and nuts of your choice (if desired).

3. Serve chilled.

Calories: 387 Fat: 8.5g Carbs: 76.4g Protein: 10g Fiber: 3.4g

Mediterranean Omelet with Wheat Bread & Blueberries

2

20 mins

7 mins

Allergy Warnings

Classification

106

Ingredients

Eggs (4, large)

Olive oil (4 tbsp, extra virgin)

Yellow onion (2 medium, chopped)

Garlic (2 cloves, minced)

Spinach (2 cups, chopped)

Tomato (1 medium, diced)

Skim milk (4 tbsp)

Kalamata olives (8, pitted and diced)

Salt and pepper (to taste)

Feta cheese (6 tbsp, crumbled)

Fresh parsley (2 tbsp, chopped)

For Serving

Whole Wheat Bread (4 slices)

Blueberries (1 cup)

Skim Milk/Coffee (2 cups)

Directions

1. Heat the oil in a pan. Add onions to the pan and fry until brown. Then, add garlic and fry for 2 minutes.

2. Add the salt, spinach, tomatoes, and cook for a few minutes. In a bowl, add egg and milk and whisk together.

3. Add the pepper and olives to the frying pan and pour the egg mixture over the sautéed vegetables.

4. Spread it around and turn up the heat so the egg cooks quickly.

5. You can lift the omelet a bit to allow the upper liquid layer to go underneath the cooked egg.

6. Continue cooking until the egg is cooked. Fold the omelet in half. Transfer to a plate, add freshly chopped parsley and cheese.

7. Serve warm with 2 slices of Whole Wheat Bread, 1/2 Cup Blueberries, and 1 Glass of Milk/Coffee.

Calories: 428 Fat: 34.5g Carbs: 23.5g Protein: 9.2g Fiber: 3.6g

Simple Mediterranean Breakfast with Sashimi & Pickles

5 15 mins 0 mins

Allergy Warnings

MILK GLUTEN FISH EGGS

Ingredients

Ricotta Cheese (1 Cup, Fresh)

Salmon (15 oz., sashimi grade, thinly sliced)

Eggs (5)

Green Olives (5)

Sourdough Rye Bread (5 Slice)

Fresh Pickles (15 Slices)

Olive Oil (3 1/3 Tsp)

Sea Salt And Fresh Black Pepper (To Taste)

Directions

1. Boil your eggs and Slice your salmon.

2. Spread the ricotta on the bread, each slice top with a sliced egg, salmon, pickle slices, and an olive.

3. Drizzle with olive oil then seasons with salt and pepper. Enjoy!

Calories: 215 **Fat:** *11g* **Carbs:** *18g* **Protein:** *12g* **Fiber:** *2g*

Italian Omelet

5 15 mins 10 mins

Allergy Warnings **Classification**

Ingredients

Mushrooms (5 Cup, Sliced)

Zucchini (5 Cup, Sliced)

Olive Oil (15 Tbsp, Divided)

Eggs (20)

Water (15 Tbsp)

Salt and Pepper

Mozzarella (2 ½ Cup)

For the Sauce:

Olive Oil (5 Tbsp)

Parsley (10 Tbsp, Chopped)

Tomato (5 Medium)

Garlic (5 cloves)

Salt (A Pinch)

Basil (2 ½ Tsp)

Directions

1. Heat 1 tbsp of olive oil in a skillet, then add the mushroom and zucchini. Sauté until brown. Set aside but keep warm.

2. In a bowl, whisk together eggs, water, salt, and pepper. Heat the skillet and add the remaining 2 tbsp oil.

3. Add the beaten eggs. Cook for a few minutes. As the eggs cook, push the uncooked portion beneath and let the top part set.

4. Once the eggs are cooked, add the vegetables over to one side and sprinkle the mozzarella cheese.

5. Fold the other half of the egg over the filling. Remove the eggs on a plate.

6. When making the sauce, heat oil. Add basil, tomatoes, parsley, and garlic. Cook thoroughly until done.

7. Serve the sauce with the omelet. Enjoy!

Calories: 773 Fat: 75g Carbs: 7g Protein: 25.3g Fiber: 2g

Lunch

Roasted Beet Salad with Ricotta Cheese

4   10 mins   1 hr

Allergy Warnings   **Classification**

Ingredients

Red beets (8.8 oz, large, wrapped in foil)

Yellow beets (8.8 oz, small, wrapped in foil)

Mesclun (4.3 oz)

Mustard Vinaigrette (4.4 oz)

Ricotta cheese (2.1 oz)

Walnuts (0.1 oz, chopped)

Directions

1. Bake at 400 F until the beets are tender, about 1 hour.

2. Cool the beets slightly. Trim the root and stem ends and pull off the peels.

3. Cut the red beets crosswise into thin slices.

4. Cut the yellow beets vertically into quarters.

5. Arrange the sliced red beets in circles on cold salad plates. Toss the mesclun with half the vinaigrette.

6. Drizzle the remaining vinaigrette over the sliced beets.

7. Place a small mound of greens in the center of each plate.

8. Arrange the quartered yellow beets around the greens.

9. Sprinkle the tops of the salads with the crumbled ricotta and walnuts (if using).

Calories: 290 Fat: 6g Carbs: 12g Protein: 6g Fiber: 3g

Baked Fish with Tomatoes and Mushrooms

4

12 mins

25 mins

Allergy Warnings

FISH

Classification

Ingredients

Fish (4, whole and small, 12 oz each)

Salt (to taste)

Pepper (to taste)

Dried thyme (pinch)

Parsley (4 sprigs)

Olive oil (as needed)

Onion (4 oz, small dice)

Shallots (1 oz, minced)

Mushrooms (8 oz, chopped)

Tomato concasse (6.4 oz)

Dry white wine (3.2 fl oz)

Directions

1. Scale and clean the fish but leave the heads on. Season the fish inside and out with salt and pepper and put a small pinch of thyme and a sprig of parsley in the cavity of each.

2. Use as many baking pans to hold the fish in a single layer. Oil the pans with a little olive oil.

3. Sauté the onions and shallots in a little olive oil for about 1 minute. Add the mushrooms and sauté lightly.

4. Put the sautéed vegetables and the tomatoes in the bottoms of the baking pans.

5. Put the fish in the pans. Oil the tops lightly. Pour in the wine.

6. Bake at 400F until the fish is done. The time will vary but will average 15-20 minutes. Base often with the liquid in the pan.

7. Remove the fish and keep them warm until they are plated.

8. Remove the vegetables from the pans with a slotted spoon and check for seasonings. Serve a spoonful of the vegetables with the fish, placing it under or alongside each fish.

9. *Continue/next page...*

9.

Strain, degrease, and reduce the cooking liquid slightly. Just before serving, moisten each portion with 1-2 tbsp of the liquid.

Calories: 350 Fat: 9g Carbs: 6g Protein: 55g Fiber: 1g

Goat Cheese and Walnut Salad

3   15 mins   10 mins

Allergy Warnings   ## Classification

GLUTEN   MILK   NUTS

Ingredients

Beet (2 oz)

Arugula (3 oz)

Bibb lettuce (2 oz)

Romaine lettuce (9 oz)

Breadcrumbs (1/4 cup, dry)

Dried thyme (1/4 tbsp)

Dried basil (1/4 tbsp)

Black pepper (1/3 tsp)

Fresh goat's milk cheese (6.35 oz, preferably in log shape)

Walnut pieces (1.1 oz)

Red wine vinaigrette (2 fl. Oz.)

Directions

1. Trim, wash, and dry all the salad greens.

2. Tear the greens into small pieces. Toss well.

3. Mix the herbs, pepper, and crumbs.

4. Slice the cheese into 1 oz pieces. In the seasoned crumbs mix, roll the pieces of cheese to coat them

5. Place the cheese on a sheet pan. Bake at the temperature of 425 F for 10 minutes.

6. At the same time, toast the walnuts in a dry sauté pan or the oven with the cheese.

7. Toss the greens with the vinaigrette and arrange on cold plates. Top each plate of greens with 2 pieces of cheese and sprinkle with walnuts.

*Calories: 460 **Fat:** 40g **Carbs:** 13g **Protein:** 17g **Fiber:** 3g*

Grilled Spiced Turkey Burger

3   15 mins   20 mins

Classification

Ingredients

Onion (1.8 oz, chopped fine)

Extra Virgin Olive Oil (1/3 tbsp)

Turkey (14.4 oz, ground)

Salt (1/3 tbsp)

Curry powder (1/3 tbsp)

Lemon zest (2/5 tsp, grated)

Pepper (1/8 tsp)

Cinnamon (1/8 tsp)

Coriander (1/4 tsp, ground)

Cumin (1/8 tsp, ground)

Cardamom (1/8 tsp, ground)

Water (1.2 fl oz)

Tomato Raisin Chutney (as desired)

Cilantro leaves (as desired)

Directions

1. Cook the onions in the oil until soft. Cool completely.

2. Combine the turkey, onions, spices, water, and salt in a bowl. Toss until mixed.

3. Divide the mixture into 5 oz portions (or as desired). Form each portion into a thick patty.

4. Broil or grill until well done, but do not overcook it, or the burger will dry.

5. Plate the burgers. Place a spoonful of chutney on top of each burger or place it on the side with a small amount of greens. You can serve the burger and garnish as a sandwich on whole-grain bread.

Calories: 250 Fat: 14g Carbs: 2g Protein: 27g Fiber: 1g

Tomato Tea Party Sandwiches

4

15 mins

0 mins

Allergy Warnings

GLUTEN

MILK

Ingredients

Whole wheat bread (4 slices)

Extra virgin olive oil (4 1/3 tbsp)

Basil (2 1/8 tbsp., minced)

Tomato slices (4 thick)

Ricotta cheese (4 oz)

Dash of pepper

Directions

1. Toast bread to your preference.

2. Spread 2 tsp. olive oil on each slice of bread. Add the cheese.

3. Top with tomato, then sprinkle with basil and pepper.

4. Serve with lemon water and enjoy it!

Calories: 239 Fat: 16.4g Carbs: 18.6g Protein: 6g Fiber: 3g

Veggie Shish Kebabs

3

10 mins

0 mins

Allergy Warnings

Classification

Ingredients

Skewers (9, wooden)

Cherry tomatoes (9)

Mozzarella balls (9 low-fat)

Basil leaves (9)

Olive oil (1 tsp.)

Zucchini (3, sliced)

Dash of pepper

For Serving:

Whole Wheat Bread (6 slices)

Directions

1. Stab 1 cherry tomato, low-fat mozzarella ball, zucchini, and basil leaf onto each skewer.

2. Place skewers on a plate and drizzle with olive oil. Finish with a sprinkle of pepper.

3. Set your bread to toast. Serve 2 bread slices with 3 kebobs.

4. Enjoy!

5.

Calories: 349 Fat: 5.7g Carbs: 61g Protein: 15g Fiber: 6.2g

Crispy Falafel

3

20 mins

8 mins

Classification

Ingredients

Chickpeas (1 cup, drained and rinsed)

Parsley (½ cup, chopped with stems removed)

Cilantro (1/3 cup, chopped with stems removed)

Dill (¼ cup, chopped with stems removed)

Cloves garlic (4, minced)

Sesame seeds (1 tbsp., toasted)

Coriander (½ tbsp.)

Black pepper (½ tbsp.)

Cumin (½ tbsp.)

Baking powder (½ tsp.)

Cayenne (½ tsp.)

Olive oil for frying

Directions

1. Thoroughly dry your chickpeas with a paper towel.

2. Place the parsley, cilantro, and dill in a food processor and pulse until it forms mulch.

3. Add in the chickpeas, garlic, coriander, black pepper, cumin, baking powder, and cayenne. Pulse this mixture until smooth and well combined.

4. Transfer the mixture to an airtight container and let it sit in the fridge for about an hour, or until stiff.

5. Remove the mixture from the refrigerator and stir in the baking powder and sesame seeds until well combined.

6. Scoop the mixture into a pan with 3 inches of olive oil over medium heat to create patties. Keep in mind as you create the patties that you are aiming to make 12 with the mixture.

7. Let the falafel patties fry for 1-2 minutes on each side or until golden brown.

8. Once your falafel patties are nicely browned, transfer them to a plate lined with paper towels to finish crisping.

9. *Continue/next page...*

9. Dip, dunk, fill, and enjoy!

Calories: 349 Fat: 5.7g Carbs: 61g Protein: 15g Fiber: 6.2g

Onion Fried Eggs

4   15 mins   31 mins

Allergy Warnings   **Classification**

EGGS   MILK

Ingredients

Eggs (11)

White mushroom (1 cup)

Feta cheese (4 oz, crumbled)

Sun-dried tomatoes (1/2 cup, chopped)

Onion (2 large, sliced)

Garlic clove (2, minced)

Olive oil (2.5 tbsp.)

Dash of pepper

Directions

1. Put a pan with the olive oil over medium-low heat.

2. Once the oil is hot, add the onions and mushrooms then stir them into the oil.

3. Allow the onion and mushroom mix to cook for about one hour, or until they become a deep brown color. Stir them every 5-7 minutes to ensure they cook evenly.

4. After the onions have browned, add the sun dried tomatoes and garlic, and let cook for 2 minutes or until fragrant.

5. Once the sun dried tomatoes and garlic are fragrant, spread all the ingredients out into an even, thin layer across the pan.

6. Crack the eggs overtop the ingredients already in the pan.

7. Sprinkle your feta cheese and pepper over top of the eggs.

8. Cover the pan with its corresponding lid and let the eggs sit to cook for about 10-12 minutes. Gently shake the pan at 10 minutes to check on the consistency of the egg yolks. Continue to cook until they reach your desired level of doneness.

9. *Continue/next page...*

9. Remove pan from heat and divide the mixture between two plates.

10. Serve, and enjoy!

Calories: 360 Fat: 27g Carbs: 10g Protein: 20g Fiber: 2g

Dinner

Pan-Smoked Trout Fillet with Pepper

3

10 mins

12 mins

Allergy Warnings

FISH

Classification

Ingredients

Trout fillet (12 oz)

Extra Virgin Olive Oil (0.25 fl oz)

Ground coriander (1/4 tsp)

Ground cumin (1/4 tsp)

Ground cloves (1/8 tsp)

Ground fennel (1/4 tsp)

Black pepper (1/4 tsp)

Salt (1/4 tsp)

Roasted pepper salad (12 oz.)

Directions

1. Cut the trout fillets into 4 oz portions.

2. Brush the trout lightly with oil.

3. Combine the spices and salt. Sprinkle over the fish to coat them in a light, even layer.

4. Set up a smoke roasting system. Heat the pan of wood chips or sawdust on top of the stove until smoke appears. Lay the trout fillets on the rack, cover, and turn the heat to medium-low. Smoke roast for 2 minutes.

5. Transfer the pan to an oven preheated to 400 F and continue roasting another 8-10 minutes, or until the fish is just cooked through.

6. Arrange the trout fillets and the pepper salad on plates. Serves immediately.

Calories: 370 Fat: 25g Carbs: 9g Protein: 29g Fiber: 2g

Pan-Smoked Spiced Chicken Breasts with Fruit Salsa

3

15 mins

20 mins

Allergy Warnings

Classification

Ingredients

Paprika (1/2 tbsp)

Ground cumin (½ tsp)

Dried thyme (1/4 tsp)

Ground coriander (½ tsp)

Salt (½ tsp)

Pepper (1/4 tsp)

Chicken breasts (3, boneless and skinless, 5 oz each)

Extra Virgin Olive Oil (as needed)

Wheatberries (9.75 oz, with Pecans and Poblanos)

Fruit Salsa (6 oz)

Cilantro sprigs (as needed, for garnish, optional)

Directions

1. Combine the cumin, paprika, thyme, salt, pepper, and coriander.

2. Coat the breast with the spice mixture.

3. Brush with oil lightly. Allow marinating, refrigerated, 3-4 hours.

4. Set up a smoke-roasting system. Heat the pan of sawdust or wood chips on the stovetop until smoke appears. Place the chicken on a rack and cover it. Turn the heat to medium. Smoke roast for 10 minutes.

5. Transfer the pan to an oven preheated to 400 F and roast for another 10 minutes.

6. For each portion, place a 3 oz portion of wheatberries on the center of a plate. Slice a chicken breast on the diagonal and arrange the slices, overlapping, on top of the wheatberries. Spoon 2 oz salsa next to the chicken and wheatberries. Garnish with cilantro.

Calories: 200 Fat: 6g Carbs: 7g Protein: 29g Fiber: 1g

Baked Chicken with Brown Rice & Veggies

3 10 mins 1 hr

Allergy Warnings

Ingredients

Whole wheat flour (1 oz)

Salt (1½ tsp)

White pepper (1/8 tsp)

Paprika (1/4 tsp)

Dried thyme (1/8 tsp)

Roma Tomato (3, large, sliced)

Broccoli (3 oz., cut in florets)

Parsley (1 bunch, stems removed)

Fryer chicken parts (30 oz.)

Extra Virgin Olive Oil (3 oz)

Brown rice (1 cup)

Water (2 cups)

Directions

1. Combine the flour and seasonings in a pan.

2. Dry the chicken pieces with paper towels if they are wet. Dredge in the seasoned flour.

3. Place the chicken in the Extra Virgin Olive Oil so that it is coated fully. Let excess drip off.

4. Place the chicken on a sheet pan, with the skin side up. If using both dark and light meat parts, place them on separate pans. Add your broccoli in around your chicken.

5. Bake the chicken at 400 F until done, about 45 mins.

6. Rinse your brown rice and set it on high heat with your water and ½ tsp salt. Cover and bring to a boil.

7. Reduce heat to a simmer and cook for 45 minutes.

8. Switch off your heat and leave covered for about 10 minutes.

9. When ready to serve. Split your rice, chicken, and tomatoes evenly and store or enjoy.

Calories: 532 Fat: 30g Carbs: 23g Protein: 39g Fiber: 1g

Tomato Basil Stuffed Peppers

6

15 mins

1 hr 11 mins

Allergy Warnings

Classification

Ingredients

Tofu (16 oz., crumbled)

Bell peppers (4, the color of your preference)

Tomato sauce (1 can)

Brown rice (1 ½ cups, cooked)

Heavy cream (1/3 cup)

Basil (¼ cup, chopped)

Feta cheese (¾ cup)

Garlic cloves (3, minced)

Onion (½, diced)

Olive oil (1 tbsp.)

Dash of pepper

Directions

1. Preheat the oven to 400 degrees Fahrenheit.

2. Slice the tops of the peppers and scoop out their insides. Discard them and set the peppers aside.

3. Put the tofu in a bowl and fold the pepper into it until evenly distributed.

4. Place the pan with the olive oil over medium heat.

5. When the oil is hot, add the onion and let it cook for about 5 minutes or until translucent.

6. Once the onion is translucent, add 2 garlic cloves and cook for 1 minute or until fragrant.

7. As soon as the garlic is fragrant, add the seasoned crumbled tofu and let it cook for 10-15 minutes or until cooked through.

8. While the tofu cooks, combine the heavy cream, and the left-over garlic clove and mix.

9. Transfer this mixture to a saucepan. Place the saucepan on low heat and stir in some basil, leaving a little bit to garnish your peppers later.

10. Stir the brown rice and feta cheese into the tofu mixture until well combined.

11. *Continue/next page...*

11. Pour half of the tomato sauce mixture into the pan and stir again until well combined. Remove from heat.

12. Line your bell peppers close together and divide the frying pan mixture between them, pouring it into each pepper until full.

13. Spoon about 2 teaspoons of the remaining cream sauce into each pepper.

14. Transfer the peppers to a baking pan and pour the remainder of the tomato sauce into the bottom of the pan.

15. Place the tops back on the peppers and stick them in the oven for 20 minutes.

16. Remove the baking pan from the oven, cover the peppers with aluminum foil.

17. Place the baking pan back in the oven and cook for an additional 30 minutes.

18. Remove the baking pan from the oven, discard the aluminum foil, and garnish with the remaining basil.

19. Place 2 peppers on each plate, serve with a glass of wine, and enjoy!

Calories: 349 Fat: 13g Carbs: 46g Protein: 14g Fiber: 5g

Chicken Paillard with Grilled Vegetables

4

12 mins

15-20 mins

Allergy Warnings

MILK

Classification

GLUTEN free

Ingredients

Chicken breast (4 boneless, skinless about 6 oz each)

Garlic cloves (1, chopped)

Fresh rosemary (1/3 tbsp, chopped)

Salt (1/4 tsp)

Pepper (1/8 tsp)

Lemon juice (1 fl oz)

Olive oil (1 fl oz)

Grilled vegetable medley (as desired)

Fresh rosemary (4 sprigs)

Directions

1. Place each chicken breast between sheets of plastic film. With a meat mallet, carefully pound to a uniform thickness of about ¼ in.

2. Combine the rosemary, garlic, pepper, and salt. Rub the flattened chicken on both sides with the mixture. Sprinkle both sides with the lemon juice, then with the olive oil. Let marinate 2-4 hours in the refrigerator.

3. Preheat a grill or broiler (very hot). Place the chicken breasts and veggies on the grill or under your broiler, skin side (that is, the side that had the skin on) down, and grill until about one-fourth has done. Rotate on the grill to mark. Continue to cook until about half has done. Turnover and continue to grill until just cooked through.

4. Plate and serve. Garnish with a sprig of rosemary.

Calories: 250 Fat: 11g Carbs: 1g Protein: 34g Fiber: 1.5g

Mediterranean Sushi

4

15 mins

0 mins

Allergy Warnings   **Classification**

Ingredients

Cucumber (12 large)

Tomatoes (36 tbsp., sun-dried, diced)

Hummus (36 tbsp.)

Feta cheese (36 tbsp., low-fat, crumbled)

Garlic (24 cloves, minced)

Dash pepper

Directions

1. Using a vegetable sheer, peel the outside skin off the cucumber.

2. Create 6 thin pieces by slicing lengthwise.

3. Lay cucumber slices out side-by-side on a cutting board.

4. Layer about 1 ½ teaspoon of hummus over each cucumber slice.

5. Top each slice with 1 ½ teaspoon sun-dried tomatoes and low-fat feta cheese.

6. Sprinkle it with pepper.

7. Pick up the end of a cucumber slice that is closest to you and begin to roll so that ingredients are on the inside. Ensure not to roll too tight or the filling will squish out.

8. Secure each roll with a toothpick.

9. Repeat steps 8-9 for the remaining slices of cucumber.

10. Plate and enjoy it!

Calories: 408 Fat: 20.4g Carbs: 36g Protein: 24g Fiber: 12g

Chunky Vegetables Soup

4   15 mins   0 mins

Classification

Ingredients

Olive oil (1¼ tbsp)

Onion (2 chopped)

Vegetable broth (7.2 cups)

Tomatoes (2¾ cups canned)

Oregano (2 tsp)

Basil (2 tsp dried)

Parsley (2 tbsp dried)

Bay leaves (7)

Carrots (4 chopped)

Butternut squash (4 diced)

Celery stalks (4, diced)

Kidney beans (4 cans, drained and rinsed)

Dash of pepper

Dash of italian seasoning

Directions

1. Heat oil in a large pot. Add onions and brown.

2. Add broth, tomatoes, basil, oregano, parsley, butternut squash, celery, carrots, and boil the mixture.

3. Turn the heat down and simmer for 15 minutes until vegetables are tender.

4. Add the beans and cook until heated through about another 3 minutes. Season with salt and pepper.

5. Serve hot with rice or bread.

Calories: 540 Fat: 10.3g Carbs: 88g Protein: 27g Fiber: 21g

Cheesy Eggplant Sandwiches

4

15 mins

12 mins

Allergy Warnings

GLUTEN

MILK

Classification

Vegetarian

Ingredients

Eggplant (3 medium-sized, diced)

Whole wheat italian bread (8 pieces)

Sun-dried tomatoes (2 cups)

Baby spinach (2 cups)

Mozzarella cheese (2/3 cup, low-fat and grated)

Parmesan cheese (4 tbsp., grated)

Basil (4 tbsp., minced)

Olive oil (3 tbsp. + 3 tsp., divided)

Directions

1. Preheat the grill to medium-high.

2. Toss diced eggplant with 1 tbsp. olive oil. Place eggplant on a baking sheet.

3. In a small bowl, mix parmesan and mozzarella.

4. Spread remaining olive oil over both sides of rustic Italian bread.

5. Dump baby spinach into a medium-sized microwave-safe bowl. Cover with a microwave-safe lid that has breathing holes.

6. Put the bowl into the microwave for 1 1/2 - 2 minutes, or until baby spinach is soft.

7. Dump sun dried tomatoes, basil, and 3 tbsp. water into a separate microwave-safe bowl. Stir and cover with a microwave-safe lid that has breathing holes.

8. Place the bowl with sun dried tomatoes, basil, and water in the microwave for about 1 1/2 minute, or until mixture is bubbling.

9. Top eggplant with microwaved baby spinach, sun-dried tomatoes, basil, and water. Make sure it is spread evenly across the baking sheet.

10. *Continue/next page...*

10. Place the baking sheet on the grill, pushing ingredients around every so often. Continue to do so until eggplant has browned on both sides.

11. Grill the rustic Italian bread until nicely toasted, about 1 minute each side.

12. Once the bread is toasted and the eggplant has browned, divide the eggplant mixture and cheeses over the bread slices.

13. With the bread slices on the baking sheet, close the grill lid and let sit about 4-6 minutes or until the cheese has melted.

14. Serve and enjoy!

Calories: 398 Fat: 19g Carbs: 49g Protein: 15g Fiber: 14g

PART 4:
BONUS RECIPES

Snack

Black Bean Cake with Salsa

20　　　　15 mins　　　　15-20 mins

Classification

Ingredients

Olive oil (1 fl oz)

Onion (16 oz, cut brunoise)

Garlic (2-4 cloves, chopped)

Jalapenos (seeded and brunoise)

Ground cumin (2 tsp)

Black beans (32 oz., cooked)

Oregano (1 tsp, dried)

Salt (to taste)

Pepper (to taste)

Salsa cruda (450 ml)

Directions

1. Heat the olive oil in a sauté pan over low heat.

2. Add the garlic and onions, cook until soft. Do not brown.

3. Add the ground cumin and jalapeno. Cook for a few more minutes.

4. Add the oregano and beans. Cook until they are heated through.

5. Place the mixture in a food processor and blend in a puree. The mixture should be thick to hold its shape. If the mixture becomes too dry, moisten with a little water.

6. Adjust the seasoning with salt and pepper if needed.

7. Divide the mixture into 2 oz portions. Form into small, flat cakes.

8. Brown the cakes lightly on both sides in hot olive oil in a sauté pan. They will be exceptionally soft; handle carefully.

9. Serve 2 cakes per portion with 1 ½ fl oz salsa.

Calories: 260   Fat: 12g   Carbs: 30g   Protein: 9g   Fiber: 9g

Pickled Apple

12 oz *(yield)*   10 mins   15-20 mins

Classification

Ingredients

Water (1/2 cup)

Maple syrup (3 ½ oz)

Cider vinegar (1/2 cup)

Sachet

Peppercorns (3-4)

Mustard seed (1/4 tsp)

Coriander seed (1/4 tsp)

Salt (1/4 tsp)

Granny smith apple (2, peeled, cored, and cut into small dice)

Italian parsley (1 tbsp, cut chiffonade)

Directions

1. Combine the water, maple syrup, vinegar, sachet, and sat in a saucepan. Bring to a boil.

2. Pour the liquid and the sachet over the apples in a nonreactive container.

3. Let it be refrigerated for 3-4 hours or overnight.

4. Drain the apples before serving and toss with the parsley.

Calories: 50 Fat: 0g Carbs: 12g Protein: 0g Fiber: 2.4g

Baked Clams Oreganata

10

30 mins

10-15 mins

Allergy Warnings

CRUSTACEANS

GLUTEN

MILK

Ingredients

Cherrystone clams (30)

Olive oil (2 fl oz)

Onions (1 oz, chopped fine)

Garlic (1 tsp, finely chopped)

Lemon juice (1 fl oz)

Fresh breadcrumbs (10 oz)

Parsley (1 tbsp, chopped)

Oregano (3/4 tsp, dried)

White pepper (1/8 tsp)

Parmesan cheese (1/3 cup)

Paprika (as needed)

Lemon wedges (10)

Directions

1. Open the clams. Catch the juice in a bowl.

2. Remove the clams from the shell. Place them in a strainer over the bowl of juice. Let them drain 15 minutes in the refrigerator. Save the 30 best half-shells.

3. Chop the clams into small pieces.

4. Heat the oil in a sauté pan. Add the onion and garlic. Sauté about 1 minute, but do not brown.

5. Use half of the clam juice, then reduce it over high heat by three-fourths.

6. Remove from the heat and add the crumbs, parsley, lemon juice, white pepper, and oregano. Mix gently to avoid making the crumbs pasty.

7. If necessary, adjust the seasonings.

8. Once the mixture has cooled. Mix in the chopped clams.

9. Place the mixture in the 30 clamshells. Sprinkle with parmesan cheese and (very lightly) with paprika.

10. Place on a sheet pan and refrigerate until needed.

11. *Continue/next page...*

11. For each order, bake 3 clams in a hot oven (450 F) until they are hot and the top brown.

12. Garnish with a lemon wedge.

Calories: 180 Fat: 8g Carbs: 16g Protein: 10g Fiber: 1g

Tuna Tartare

8

15 mins

0 mins

Allergy Warnings

FISH

Classification

GLUTEN free

Ingredients

Sashimi quality tuna (26.5 g, well-trimmed)

Shallots (1 oz, minced)

Parsley (2 tbsp, chopped)

Fresh tarragon (2 tbsp, chopped)

Lime juice (2 tbsp)

Dijon-style mustard (1 fl oz)

Olive oil (2 fl oz)

Salt (to taste)

White pepper (to taste)

Directions

1. Use a knife to mince the tuna.

2. Mixed the rest of the ingredients with the chopped tuna before serving.

3. Season to taste with pepper and salt.

Calories: 200 Fat: 12g Carbs: 2g Protein: 21g Fiber: 1g

Cod Cakes

12

30 mins

25 mins

Allergy Warnings

FISH

GLUTEN

EGGS

Ingredients

Cod (12 oz, cooked)

Turnips puree (12 oz.)

Whole eggs (2 ½ oz, beaten)

Egg yolk (1 yolk, beaten)

Salt (to taste)

White pepper (to taste)

Ground ginger (pinch)

Standard Breading Procedure:

Whole wheat flour (as needed)

Egg wash (as needed)

Breadcrumbs (as needed)

Tomatoes sauce (as desired)

Directions

1. Flake the fish until it is well shredded.

2. Combine with the turnips, egg, and egg yolk.

3. Season to taste with salt, pepper, and a little ground ginger.

4. Scale the mixture into 2 ½ oz portions. Shape the mixture into a ball, then slightly flattened the mixture cakes.

5. Put the mixture through the Standard Breading Procedure.

6. Deep-fry at 350 F until golden brown.

7. Serve 2 cakes per portion. Accompany with tomato sauce.

Calories: 280 Fat: 6g Carbs: 33g Protein: 23g Fiber: 2g

Grilled Vegetable Kebabs

12

12 mins

8-15 mins

Classification

Ingredients

Zucchini (6 oz, trimmed)

Yellow Summer Squash (6 oz, trimmed)

Bell pepper (6 oz, red or orange, cut into 1 ½ in. squares)

Onion (12 oz, red, large dice)

Mushroom caps (12, medium)

Olive oil (12 fl oz)

Garlic (1/2 oz, crushed)

Rosemary (1 ½ tsp, dried)

Thyme (1/2 tsp, dried)

Salt (2 tsp)

Black pepper (1/2 tsp)

Directions

1. Cut the zucchini and yellow squash into 12 equal slices each.

2. Arrange the vegetables on 12 bamboo skewers. Give each skewer an equal arrangement of vegetable pieces.

3. Place the skewers in a single layer in a hotel pan.

4. Mix the oil, garlic, herbs, salt, and pepper to make a marinade.

5. Pour the marinade over the vegetables, turning them to coat completely.

6. Marinate 1 hour. Turn the skewers once or twice during margination to ensure the vegetables are coated.

7. Remove the skewers from the marinade and let the excess oil drip off.

Calories: 50 Fat: 3g Carbs: 5g Protein: 1g Fiber: 1g

Vegetable Fritters

10

15 mins

36 mins

Allergy Warnings

EGGS

GLUTEN

MILK

Classification

Vegetarian

Ingredients

Egg (3, beaten)

Milk (8 fl oz)

Whole wheat flour (8 oz)

Baking powder (1 tbsp)

Salt (½ tsp)

Maple syrup (1/2 oz)

Vegetables:

Carrot (12 oz, diced, cooked)

Baby lima beans (12 oz, cooked)

Asparagus (12 oz, diced, cooked)

Celery (12 oz, diced, cooked)

Turnip (12 oz, diced, cooked)

Eggplant (12 oz, diced, cooked)

Cauliflower (12 oz, diced, cooked)

Zucchini (12 oz, diced, cooked)

Parsnips (12 oz, diced, cooked)

Directions

1. Combine the eggs and milk.

2. Mix the flour, baking powder, salt, and maple syrup. Add to the milk and eggs and mix until smooth.

3. Let the batter stand for several hours in a refrigerator.

4. Stir the cold, cooked vegetables into the batter.

5. Drop with a No. 24 scoop into deep fat at 350 F. Toss the content from the scoop carefully in the hot oil. Fry until golden brown.

6. Drain well and serve.

Calories: 140 Fat: 6g Carbs: 19g Protein: 1g Fiber: 1g

Fruit and Nut Snack Mix

10

15 mins

36 mins

Allergy Warnings

Classification

Ingredients

Olive oil (1 tbsp.)

Honey (1/4 cup)

Almond extract (1 tsp.)

Ground cinnamon (1 tsp.)

Old-fashioned oats (2 cups)

Almonds (½ cup)

Dried banana chips (½ cup)

Tropical fruit mix (½ cup)

Raisins (½ cup)

Directions

1. Preheat the oven to 350 degrees.

2. In a saucepan, melt butter. Add honey, almond extract, and cinnamon. Mix well. Add oats and stir.

3. Prepare a baking pan by lining it with parchment paper.

4. Transfer the sticky oat mixture to the baking pan and spread it evenly. It should be no more than about 1 inch thick.

5. Bake for 10 minutes. Stir in almonds and bake for 5 minutes. Remove from the oven. Add the bananas, fruits, and raisins. Cool completely before serving.

Calories: 370 Fat: 11.8g Carbs: 64g Protein: 7g Fiber: 6g

Dessert

Sweet-Baked Banana

5

15 mins

20 mins

Classification

Ingredients

Bananas (6 ripe)

Honey (4 tbsp.)

Cinnamon (3 ¾ tsp.)

Directions

1. Preheat the oven to 350 degrees Fahrenheit.

2. Slice bananas into bite-sized chunks.

3. Pour honey and cinnamon into a medium-sized bowl. Mix until cinnamon is evenly spread through the honey.

4. Add bananas and gently toss until they have an even coating.

5. Transfer bananas onto a lined baking sheet. Spread them into one even layer.

6. Place the baking sheet into the oven and bake for 10-15 minutes or until bananas are slightly browned.

7. Portion into 2 bowls and enjoy!

Calories: 181 *Fat:* 0.5g *Carbs:* 48g *Protein:* 2g *Fiber:* 5g

Walnut Crescent Cookies

  10

  30 mins

  20 mins

Allergy Warnings

Classification

Ingredients

Dough:

Whole wheat flour (2 cups)

Corn oil (1 cup)

Dry white wine (½ cup)

Honey (¼ cup)

Filling:

Walnuts (1 cup, diced)

Apple (1, shredded)

Maple syrup (2 tbsp.)

Whole wheat bread crumbs (2 tbsp.)

Strawberry jam (1 tbsp.)

Cinnamon (½ tsp.)

Splenda for dusting

Directions

1. Put the corn oil and honey in a large bowl and stir together until well combined.

2. Add the dry white wine and whole wheat flour. Beat this in until a dough is formed.

3. Once dough forms, remove it from the bowl and knead it over a flat surface until soft, but not sticky. Then, let the dough sit for 30 minutes.

4. While the dough sits, you can begin to prepare the filling. Start by putting the walnuts, apple, maple syrup, whole wheat bread crumbs, strawberry jam, and cinnamon in a large bowl.

5. Mix all the ingredients until well combined. Set aside.

6. Preheat the oven to 350 degrees Fahrenheit.

7. Once half of an hour has passed, flatten the dough out over a floured flat surface until it is 1/5 of an inch thick.

8. Using a glass cup, cut circles out of the dough.

9. Set the circles aside, roll the remaining dough out again and repeat step 7 until little or no dough is left.

10. *Continue/next page...*

10. Once all of your dough has been cut into circles, divide the filling between them, dolloping a little bit in the center of each.

11. Fold each circle in half over the top of the filling and squish the edges nicely into one another so that none of the filling can seep out.

12. Line a baking sheet with parchment paper and spread the crescents out over the top.

13. Place the baking sheet in the oven and let the crescents bake for 20 minutes.

14. After 20 minutes, remove the baking sheet from the oven.

15. Dust with Splenda.

16. Serve and enjoy!

Calories: 408 Fat: 30g Carbs: 30g Protein: 6g Fiber: 2.1g

Traditional Ekmek Kataifi

 10   30 mins   20 mins

Allergy Warnings   **Classification**

EGGS NUTS MILK

Ingredients

Pastry:

Kataifi dough (1 cup)

Pistachios (1/3 cup, diced)

Olive oil (½ cup)

Syrup:

Water (¾ cup)

Honey (¾ cup)

Cinnamon (1 stick)

Strawberry puree (1/4 cup)

Lemon zest (½ tbsp.)

Custard:

Milk (3 cups, cold)

Maple syrup (2/3 cup)

Olive oil (1/3 cup)

Corn starch (1/3 cup)

Egg yolks (4)

Vanilla extract (½ tsp.)

Directions

1. Preheat the oven to 340 degrees Fahrenheit.

2. Knead the Kataifi dough, spreading apart the clumped together strands to create a fluffier consistency.

3. Spray a baking dish with cooking spray and press the Kataifi dough into the bottom of it, forming one even layer.

4. Pour the olive oil over the top and place the baking dish in the oven for 30-40 minutes, or until it is light brown.

5. While the Kataifi is in the oven, you can begin to prepare your custard. Start by placing half of the sugar and all the egg yolks in a bowl, whisking them together until well combined and bubbly. Set the mixture aside for later.

6. In a separate bowl, whisk together 4 tbsp. of milk and the corn starch until well combined. Set this mixture aside for later as well.

7. Pour the remaining milk into a large non-stick pan over high heat along with the sugar and vanilla extract. Stir this together well and bring the mixture to a boil.

8. Remove the pan from the heat as soon as the milk begins to boil. Set aside.

9. *Continue/next page...*

9. Pour 1/3 of the pan's mixture into the egg yolk mixture and whisk it in until well combined.

10. Transfer the egg yolk mixture back into the pan and place the pan back overheat, but this time on medium.

11. Whisk continuously while cooking is in progress until the mixture becomes all thick, smooth, and deliciously creamy.

12. Once the mixture is thick and rich, remove it again from the heat.

13. Add the olive oil to the pan and stir it into the mixture until melted and well combined.

14. Transfer this mixture into a baking tray and place some plastic wrap over the top of it. Ensure the plastic wrap touches the mixture to ensure it stays creamy.

15. Set this aside, let it cool, and while you're going strong, begin to prepare the syrup.

16. Stir the water, maple syrup, strawberry puree, lemon zest, and cinnamon stick together in a small pot or saucepan over medium heat until the sugar has dissolved.

17. Bring the mixture to a boil and let it boil for 3 minutes until it thickens into a syrup consistency.

18. *Continue/next page...*

18. Once it's thick enough, remove it from the heat and let it cool until it's just warm enough for you to eat it without burning your mouth.

19. By now your Kataifi dough should have been removed from the oven and cooled. If this is not the case, wait until it is cool.

20. Once the Kataifi is cool, ladle the syrup over the top one at a time, giving each spoonful enough time to be absorbed. Then, set it aside to cool completely.

21. Spread the creamy custard atop the Kataifi in a nice, even layer.

22. Sprinkle the chopped pistachios over the entire thing. You can be as creative as you like! Make a smiley face or a rainbow to impress your friends.

23. Slice into 12 pieces, serve, and enjoy!

Calories: 367 Fat: 19.5g Carbs: 45g Protein: 6g Fiber: 2g

Flaky Coconut Pie

12   30 mins   45 mins

Allergy Warnings   **Classification**

EGGS   NUTS

Ingredients

Filo pastry (11 sheets)

Coconut cream (400 ml)

Cashew (½ cup, chopped)

Honey (½ cup)

Coconut oil (¼ cup)

Coconut (¼ cup, shredded, unsweetened)

Eggs (2)

Vanilla extract (1 tsp.)

Directions

1. Preheat the oven to 350 degrees F.

2. Grease a pie dish with just enough coconut oil to cover it.

3. In a medium-size bowl, whisk together the coconut cream, honey, eggs, and vanilla until all ingredients are well combined and the sugar has dissolved. Set this aside for later.

4. Pulse the cashews and shredded coconut in a food processor until it turns into mulch. Set this aside as well.

5. Place a piece of the filo pastry on a clean, stable surface and brush a generous amount of coconut oil over it.

6. Roughly scrunch the piece of filo pastry up and place it in the pie dish.

7. Repeat steps 5-6 until the baking tray is full.

8. Once your pie dish is full, pour the coconut cream mixture over top, making sure each inch of the pastry gets soaked in it.

9. Once you're out of your coconut cream mixture, sprinkle the cashew mixture over top.

10. *Continue/next page...*

10. Place the pie dish in the oven and let it bake for 25-35 minutes or until the top has turned a nice golden-brown and the pastry has risen.

11. Remove the baking tray from the oven and allow your pie to cool for 15 minutes.

12. Slice into 8 wedges and enjoy!

Calories: 385 Fat: 28g Carbs: 31g Protein: 6g Fiber: 5g

Ricotta Cheese Fruit Bake

6   30 mins   1 hr 10 mins

Allergy Warnings   **Classification**

EGGS   NUTS

Ingredients

Ricotta Cheese:

Ricotta cheese (1 ½ cups)

Egg (1)

Honey (3 tbsp.)

Lemon zest (1 tsp.)

Fruit Syrup:

Raspberries (1 cup, diced)

Honey (3 tbsp.)

Orange juice (2 tbsp.)

Orange blossom water (1 tsp.)

Directions

1. Place ricotta cheese in a coffee filter-lined strainer and place this in the fridge to drain overnight. Ensure the filter is placed over a container so that the drained mixture is contained.

2. Once your ricotta cheese has drained, preheat the oven to 400 degrees F.

3. Spray 6 small heat-proof bowls with cooking spray.

4. Place the drained ricotta, egg, honey, and lemon in a bowl and beat together until well combined.

5. Divide the ricotta mixture between your 6 greased bowls and place them in the oven for 30-35 minutes, or until they have turned a nice golden-brown color.

6. Then, remove them from the oven and allow them to cool.

7. While your ricotta cheese bowls are cooling, you can begin to prepare the fruit sauce. Start by placing the raspberries, honey, and orange juice in a small pot or saucepan over medium-high heat. As it starts to boil, stir so that ingredients are well combined and the sugar dissolves.

8. *Continue/next page...*

8. Once the mixture starts to boil, reduce the heat to medium-low and continue to cook, stirring occasionally, for 20-25 minutes or until the raspberries are tender and the mixture takes on a syrupy consistency.

9. Remove the mixture from the heat and stir in the orange blossom water until well combined. Then, let the mixture cool a little.

10. Once the ricotta cheese bowls have cooled, divide the fruit syrup over them.

11. Serve and enjoy!

Calories: 153 **Fat:** *6g* **Carbs:** *19g* **Protein:** *8g* **Fiber:** *0.1g*

Anginetti Lemon Cookies

6

30 mins

1 hr 10 mins

Allergy Warnings

EGGS

GLUTEN

Classification

Vegetarian

SUGAR free

Ingredients

Cookies:

Whole wheat flour (2/3 cup)

Egg (1)

Maple syrup (2 ½ tbsp.)

Olive oil (2 tbsp.)

Baking powder (2/3 tsp.)

Vanilla extract (2/3 tsp.)

Lemon zest (1/3 tsp., grated)

Icing:

Stevia (1/2 cup, sifted)

Lemon juice (2 tsp.)

Water (2 tsp.)

Olive oil (1 tsp.)

Vanilla extract (1/3 tsp.)

Directions

1. Preheat the oven to 350 degrees F.

2. Prepare a baking sheet by lining it with foil.

3. Start with the cookies. Beat together the maple syrup, olive oil, vanilla extract, and lemon zest together until ingredients are well combined.

4. Crack the egg into the mixture and beat it in as well. Then, set this mixture aside for later.

5. In a separate bowl, stir together the whole wheat flour and baking powder until well combined.

6. Gradually add this to the wet mixture, beating it in as you go.

7. Once your cookie dough is smooth and lump-free, begin to dollop it out onto the lined baking sheet. You should be able to get 12 cookies out of the mixture.

8. Place the baking sheet into the oven and bake for 10-12 minutes or until they become a nice golden-brown color.

9. While the cookies are in the oven, you can begin to prepare the icing. Start by putting the olive oil in a small pot or saucepan over medium heat.

10. _Continue/next page..._

10. Once the oil has heated, add in the maple syrup, lemon juice, water, and vanilla extract, stirring ingredients into the oil until well combined. Add a little more water to the icing if it seems too thick.

11. Once the cookies are done, brush the lemon icing over the top while they're still hot.

12. After you have applied the icing, allow the cookies to cool.

13. Once the cookies are cool, serve, and enjoy!

Calories: 104 Fat: 3g Carbs: 18g Protein: 1.2g Fiber: 0.2g

Toasted Almond Biscotti

20 20 mins 35 mins

Allergy Warnings   **Classification**

Ingredients

Whole wheat flour (1 ¼ cups)

Maple syrup (½ cup)

Almonds (1/3 cup, toasted and chopped)

Eggs (2 small)

Egg wash (1 small egg, beaten with ½ tbsp. water)

Sesame seeds (2 ½ tbsp., toasted)

Orange flower water (1 tbsp.)

Anise seeds (1 tsp.)

Baking powder (¾ tsp.)

Vanilla extract (½ tsp.)

Almond extract (¼ tsp.)

Directions

1. In a medium-sized bowl, mix the almond extract, maple syrup, orange flower water, almonds, vanilla extract, anise seeds, and 2 tbsp. sesame seeds until well combined.

2. Once all ingredients are well combined, crack the 2 eggs into the mixture and beat them in until thoroughly distributed.

3. Gradually beat in the flour and baking powder until a dough forms.

4. Place this dough in the fridge so to cool for 30 minutes.

5. Now, preheat the oven to 350 degrees F.

6. Coat your hands and a clean, stable surface with flour and knead the dough into a rectangular loaf.

7. Transfer this loaf to a baking sheet and brush the egg-water over it until the entire loaf is covered.

8. Then, coat the outside with your remaining sesame seeds.

9. Place the loaf in the oven and let it bake for about 15 minutes, or until it begins to turn a light gold color.

10. *Continue/next page...*

10. Transfer the loaf from the oven to a cooling rack. Leave to cool for about 15 minutes. Don't turn the oven off!

11. Once your loaf is cool enough to touch, slice it into 20 pieces and arrange them, cut side down, on another lined baking sheet.

12. Place the baking sheet back in the oven and let the biscotti's bake for another 15-20 minutes, or until they have turned a nice golden-brown color.

13. Remove the baking pan from the oven, let the cookies cool, and enjoy with some tea or coffee!

Calories: 74 Fat: 2.5g Carbs: 11.4g Protein: 2.5g Fiber: 1.3g

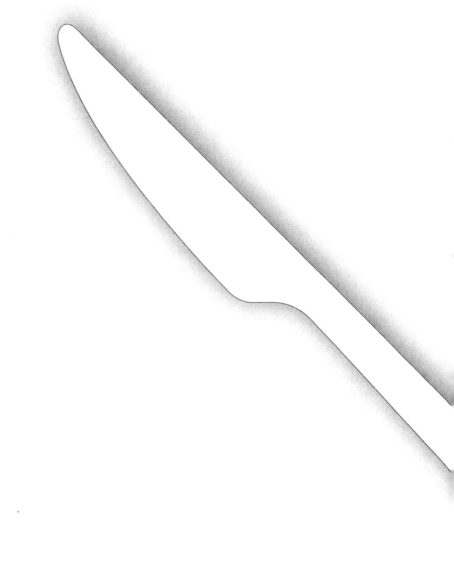

Greek Rice Pudding

12

15 mins

35 mins

Allergy Warnings

Classification

Ingredients

Full-fat milk (2 1/3 cups)

Rice (3 tbsp.)

Honey (3 tbsp.)

Corn flour (½ tbsp.)

Cold water (1 tsp.)

Directions

1. Put a pot with the milk over medium-high heat and cook until it comes to a boil.

2. Reduce the heat to medium-low and stir in the rice and honey until well combined. Keep stirring until the sugar is completely dissolved.

3. Once the sugar has dissolved, turn the heat down to low and let the mixture cook for 20-30 minutes, or until the rice has cooked.

4. Once the rice is cooked and tender, mix the corn flour and water in a small bowl until a smooth yet runny paste forms. Use more water if needed.

5. Add the corn flour mixture to the pot and stir it in until well combined.

6. Let the pudding simmer, stirring constantly, until it reaches your desired consistency.

7. Remove from heat, divide between two bowls, and serve!

Calories: 52 Fat: 1.6g Carbs: 8g Protein: 1.8g Fiber: 0.4g

Sauce

Tomato Sauce

2 L *(yield)*

15 mins

1 ½ - 2 hrs

Classification

Ingredients

Salt pork (2 oz)

Onion (4 oz, medium dice)

Carrot (4 oz, medium dice)

Tomatoes (2 L, fresh, coarsely chopped)

Tomatoes puree (1 L, canned)

Hambones (8 oz,)

Sachet

Garlic (1 clove, crushed)

Bay leaf (1/2)

Thyme (1/8 tsp, dried)

Rosemary (1/8 tsp, dried)

Peppercorns (1/8 tsp, crushed)

Salt (to taste)

Directions

1. Render the salt pork in a heavy saucepan, but do not brown it.

2. Add the onion and carrots and sauté until slightly softened, but do not brown.

3. Add the tomatoes and their juice, tomatoes puree, bone s, and sachet. Bring the content to a boil, reduce the heat to a simmer for 1 ½ - 2 hours.

4. Remove both the bones and sachet. Strain the sauce.

5. Adjust the seasoning with sugar and salt.

6. Evaluate the finished sauce.

Calories: 20   Fat: 1g   Carbs: 3g   Protein: 1g   Fiber: 1g

Ancho Sauce

25.6 oz *(yield)*   10 mins   3 mins

Classification

Ingredients

Ancho chiles (8, dried)

Onion (2 oz, chopped)

Garlic (3 cloves, chopped)

Ground cumin (1 tsp)

Oregano (1/2 tsp, dried)

Water (2 cups)

Olive Oil (1 fl. Oz.)

Salt (to taste)

Directions

1. Toast the chiles lightly in a dry skillet until softened. Split open. Remove and discard seeds and core.

2. Soak the chiles about 30 minutes in enough hot water to cover. Drain.

3. Add chiles, water, garlic, onion, cumin, and oregano, in a blender. Blend until it is a smooth puree.

4. Heat the oil in a saucepan and add the chile purée. Simmer for 2 -3 minutes.

5. Season to taste with salt.

Calories: 30 Fat: 1.5g Carbs: 3g Protein: 1g Fiber: 1g

Miso Sauce

12 fl oz *(yield)*   8 mins   0 mins

Classification

Ingredients

Miso (8 oz)

Maple syrup (2 ½ oz)

Mirin (2 fl oz, sweet Japanese rice wine)

Directions

1. Over low heat toast the sesame seeds in a dry sauté pan until aromatic and slightly darkened.

2. Grind the toasted seeds in a mortar or spice grinder.

3. Mix with the remaining ingredients. Stir well.

Calories: 110 Fat: 3g Carbs: 15g Protein: 3g Fiber: 1g

Chili Barbecue Sauce

4 ½ cups *(yield)*   10 mins   20 mins

Allergy Warnings   **Classification**

Ingredients

Bottled chili sauce (2 ½ cups)

Soy sauce (8 fl oz)

Dark honey (2 oz)

Worcestershire sauce (1 ½ fl oz)

Water (2 cups)

Lemon juice (6 fl oz)

Hot red pepper sauce (1 tbsp)

Whole chipotle chiles (2)

Chili powder (3 tbsp)

Directions

1. Combine all ingredients in a heavy saucepan. Bring to a boil.

2. Simmer for 15 minutes.

3. Strain.

4. Adjust seasoning with salt if necessary. It is not likely more salt will be needed; soy sauce is salty.)

Calories: 35 Fat: 0g Carbs: 8g Protein: 1g Fiber: 1g

Dressing

Emulsified French Dressing

 1 qt *(yield)*   10 mins   0 mins

Allergy Warnings

EGGS

Classification

Ingredients

Egg (1, preferably pasteurized)

Salt (1 ½ tsp)

Paprika (1 ½ tsp)

Mustard (1 ½ tsp, dry)

White pepper (1/4 tsp)

Salad oil (2 ½ cups)

Cider vinegar (4 fl oz)

Lemon juice (2 fl oz)

Vinegar (as needed)

Directions

1. Place the eggs in a mixer bowl and mix it until well beaten.

2. Add all the dry ingredients into the bowl. Mix until fully combined.

3. Turn the mixer to high speed then pour the oil slowly.

4. If the mix is too thick then use a little vinegar to thin it out.

5. Beat in the lemon juice.

6. The dressing should be pourable, not thick like mayonnaise. If it is too thick, taste for seasoning first. If the dressing is not tart enough, thin with a little vinegar or lemon juice. If it is tart enough, thin with water.

Calories: 190 Fat: 21g Carbs: 0g Protein: 0g Fiber: 0g

Caesar Dressing

 1 qt *(yield)*   10 mins   0 mins

Allergy Warnings **Classification**

EGGS   FISH   MILK

Ingredients

Anchovy fillet (25)

Garlic (2 tsp, crushed)

Egg (4, pasteurized)

Lemon juice (6 fl oz)

Olive oil (2 ½ cups)

Parmesan cheese (2 oz, grated)

Salt (to taste)

Directions

1. Mash the anchovies and garlic together to make a paste.

2. Place the eggs in a mixer bowl and mix until well beaten.

3. Add half of the lemon juice, anchovy, and garlic paste. Whip until well mixed.

4. With the mixer on high speed, pour the oil slowly.

5. If the mix is too thick then use a little of the remaining lemon juice.

6. When the dressing becomes thick, add a little of the remaining lemon juice.

7. Mix in the rest of the oil and the lemon juice.

8. Mix in the parmesan cheese and salt.

Calories: 170 Fat: 18g Carbs: 1g Protein: 2g Fiber: 0g

Cooked Salad Dressing

1 L *(yield)*

10 mins

0 mins

Allergy Warnings

EGGS   GLUTEN   MILK

Classification

Vegetarian

Ingredients

Maple syrup (2 oz)

Whole wheat flour (2 oz)

Salt (1 tbsp)

Mustard (1 tbsp, dry)

Cayenne (1/8 tsp)

Eggs (2)

Eggs yolk (2)

Milk (2 ½ cups)

Olive oil (2 oz)

Cider vinegar (6 fl oz)

Directions

1. Mix the maple syrup, flour, salt, mustard, and cayenne in a stainless-steel bowl.

2. Add the eggs and yolks and beat until smooth.

3. Place the milk in a saucepan and bring to a simmer. Be careful not to scorch it.

4. Slowly pour in half of the milk into the egg mixture and mix until it is combined. Then return the mixture into the saucepan.

5. Cook the content over low heat, stirring often. Cook until the content is thick, and it does not have a raw flour taste.

6. Remove from heat and stir in the oil. Then stir in the vinegar.

7. Immediately transfer the dressing to a stainless-steel container. Cover and cool.

Calories: 76 Fat: 5g Carbs: 6g Protein: 3g Fiber: 0g

Low Fat Buttermilk Dressing

1 L *(yield)*

10 mins

0 mins

Allergy Warnings

MILK

Classification

Vegetarian

GLUTEN free

Ingredients

Greek yogurt (2 cups, low fat, unflavored)

Buttermilk (8 fl oz)

Dijon mustard (1 tbsp)

Wine vinegar (1 fl oz)

Lemon juice (1 fl oz)

Worcestershire sauce (1 fl oz)

Parsley (1 ½ tbsp, chopped)

Garlic (1 tsp, finely chopped)

Shallots (1/2 oz, chopped fine)

Celery seed (1/2 tsp)

Maple syrup (4 tsp)

Salt (to taste)

Pepper (to taste)

Directions

1. Mix all ingredients until uniformly blended.

2. Chill at least 20 minutes to let flavors meld before serving.

3. Serve as a salad dressing or light dip.

*Calories: 15 **Fat:** 0g **Carbs:** 3g **Protein:** 1g **Fiber:** 0g*

Conclusion

Thank you for sticking with me to the end of this Mediterranean Diet Meal Prep Cookbook. I sincerely hope that the information, tips, and recipes provided were able to assist you in enjoying Mediterranean meals that are ready to go.

Please note that the meal plans presented in this book are simply meant to get you started in your first month. Once you have gotten through that, feel free to mix and match the recipes featured in the recipe sections of this book to create new and exciting meal plans.

If you enjoyed what you read through, **please take a moment to drop me a review on Amazon with your feedback**. Let me know what worked for you or if any of the tips I shared was helpful to you in any way.

Have a wonderful rest of the day.

- Lisa Rainolds

Measurement Conversion

WEIGHT CONVERSION

METRIC	CUPS	OUNCES
15g	1 tbs	1/2 ounce
30g	1/8 cup	1 ounce
60g	1/4 cup	2 ounces
115g	1/2 cup	4 ounces
170g	3/4 cup	6 ounces
225g	1 cup	16 ounces
450g	2 cups	

OVEN TEMPERATURE

CELSIUS	FAHRENHEIT
95°C	200°F
130°C	250°F
150°C	300°F
160°C	325°F
175°C	350°F
190°C	375°F
200°C	400°F
230°C	450°F

LENGHT

METRIC	IMPERIAL
3mm	1/8 inch
6mm	1/4 inch
2.5cm	1 inch
3cm	1 & 1/4 inch
5cm	2 inches
10cm	4 inches
15cm	6 inches
20cm	8 inches
22.5cm	9 inches
25cm	10 inches
28cm	11 inches

VOLUME CONVERSION

METRIC	CUPS	OUNCES
15 ml	1 tbs	1/2 fl. oz.
30 ml	2 tbs	1 fl. oz.
60 ml	1/4 cup	2 fl. oz.
125 ml	1/2 cup	4 fl. oz.
180 ml	3/4 cup	6 fl. oz.
250 ml	1 cup	16 fl. oz.
500 ml	2 cups	16 fl. oz.
1000 ml	4 cups	16 quart

About the Author

Lisa Rainolds is a Registered Nutritionist-Dietitian in Italy. Shortly after taking and passing the licensure examination for Nutritionist-Dietitians, she pursued a Diploma in Culinary Arts, becoming also a certified chef.

She decided to supplement her license with a study in the culinary arts because she believes that it will help her harness the best of her knowledge with real-world applications that can help people. These two passions form part and parcel of her professional life, and she is excited to work with any project that involves food, nutrition, fitness, and health.

Working as a freelancer for almost four years now, she's currently a TOP RATED PLUS author for different blogs and ghostwriter for some of the most well-known bestseller cookbooks. But now, the time has come to start her own lines of books!

References

What is a Mediterranean diet? (n.d.). Retrieved from https://www.nhs.uk/live-well/eat-well/what-is-a-mediterranean-diet/

62 Healthy Recipes to Cook While You're on the Mediterranean Diet. (n.d.). Retrieved from https://www.cookinglight.com/cooking-101/mediterranean-diet-recipes

Champion, L. (2017, October 30). 40 Mediterranean Diet Dinner Recipes You Can Make in 30 Minutes or Less. Retrieved from https://www.purewow.com/food/mediterranean-diet-dinner-recipes

Gisslen, W. (2015). Essentials of Professional Cooking, 2nd Edition. John Wiley & Sons.

Mediterranean diet for heart health. (2019, June 21). Retrieved from https://www.mayoclinic.org/healthy-lifestyle/nutrition-and-healthy-eating/in-depth/mediterranean-diet/art-20047801

Mediterranean diet: A guide and 7-day meal plan. (n.d.). Retrieved from https://www.medicalnewstoday.com/articles/324221

Mediterranean recipes. (n.d.). Retrieved from https://www.bbcgoodfood.com/recipes/collection/mediterranean-recipes

Suzy, & Aneesa. (2020, May 08). 50 Top Mediterranean Diet Recipes. Retrieved from https://www.themediterraneandish.com/best-mediterranean-diet-recipes/

Traditional Med Diet. (n.d.). Retrieved from https://oldwayspt.org/traditional-diets/mediterranean-diet/traditional-med-diet

What is the Mediterranean Diet? (n.d.). Retrieved from https://www.heart.org/en/healthy-living/healthy-eating/eat-smart/nutrition-basics/mediterranean-diet

Nutrition and Healthy Eating https://www.mayoclinic.org/healthy-lifestyle/nutrition-and-healthy-eating/in-depth/mediterranean-diet/art-20047801

Health Benefits of the Mediterranean diet https://academic.oup.com/biomedgerontology/article/73/3/318/4736301

The absolute Beginner's guide to meal prep https://www.thekitchn.com/how-to-meal-prep-beginner-261658

Meal Prep: a helpful healthy eating strategy https://www.hsph.harvard.edu/nutritionsource/2017/03/20/meal-prep-planning/

Index

Table Of Contents	*7*
Your FREE Gift	*11*
Introduction	***15***
How To Use The Mediterranean diet Meal Prep Cookbook	*16*
Overview About What's in the Book	*17*
Symbols to Be Aware of Throughout The Book	*18*
PART 1: **LIFESTYLE**	*21*
Chapter 1: Mediterranean diet Overview	**21**
Guidelines & Principles	21
Benefits of the Mediterranean Diet	*23*
The Mediterranean Food Pyramid	*27*
Foods You Can Enjoy	*28*
PART 2: **LET'S START**	*31*
Chapter 2: Meal Prep 101	**31**
Meal Prep Benefits	*31*
Meal Prep Principles	*33*
Types of Meal Prep	*37*
Chapter 3: Food Storage Solutions	**38**
Container Types	*38*
Freezer & Refrigerator Guidelines	*41*
Reheating and Thawing Guidelines	*43*
Top 5 Meal Prep Helpful Apps	*44*

Chapter 4: Getting Started With Meal Prep — 47

Meal Prep Equipment — 47

Grocery Shopping Tips — 52

The Best Food to Meal Prep — 55

Top 13 Mediterranean Staples — 56

10 Steps to Successful Meal Prepping — 58

Chapter 5: Mix & Match Healthy Meals — 61

How to Mix & Match Healthy Meals — 61

Master Your Portions — 65

Understanding the Essential Macros — 67

Customizing Your Meal Plan — 69

PART 3: FOUR WEEKS MEAL PLAN — 71

Chapter 6: Week 1 — 71

Meal Plan — 71

Shopping List — 72

Step by Step Prep — 75

Chapter 7: Week 2 — 78

Meal Plan — 78

Shopping List — 79

Step by Step Prep — 81

Chapter 8: Week 3 — 83

Meal Plan — 83

Shopping List — 84

Step by Step Prep — 86

Chapter 9: Week 4   *88*

Meal Plan   *88*

Shopping List   *89*

Step by Step Prep   *91*

Chapter 10: Meal Plan Recipes   *93*

Breakfast   *95*

Kickstart Your Day Berry Smoothie   *96*

Buckwheat Pancakes   *98*

Breakfast Couscous   *100*

Oatmeal with Fruits & Nuts   *102*

Greek Yogurt Bowl   *104*

Mediterranean Omelet with Wheat Bread & Blueberries   *106*

Simple Mediterranean Breakfast With Sashimi & Pickles   *108*

Italian Omelet   *110*

Lunch   *113*

Roasted Beet Salad with Ricotta Cheese   *114*

Baked Fish with Tomatoes and Mushrooms   *116*

Goat Cheese and Walnut Salad   *120*

Grilled Spiced Turkey Burger   *122*

Tomato Tea Party Sandwiches   *124*

Veggie Shish Kebabs   *126*

Crispy Falafel   *128*

Onion Fried Eggs   *132*

Dinner   *137*

Pan-Smocked Trout Fillet with Pepper Salad	*138*
Pan-smocked Spiced Chicken Breasts with Fruit Salsa	*140*
Baked Chicken with Brown Rice & Veggies	*142*
Tomato Basil Stuffed Peppers	*144*
Chicken Paillard with Grilled Vegetables	*148*
Mediterranean Sushi	*150*
Chunky Vegetable Soup	*152*
Cheesy Eggplant Sandwiches	*154*

PART 4: BONUS RECIPES — *158*

Snack — *159*

Black Bean Cake with Salsa	*160*
Pickled Apple	*162*
Baked Clams Oreganata	*164*
Tuna Tartare	*168*
Cod Cakes	*170*
Grilled Vegetable Kebabs	*172*
Vegetable Fritters	*174*
Fruit and Nut Snack Mix	*176*

Dessert — *179*

Sweet-Baked Banana	*180*
Walnut Crescent Cookies	*182*
Traditional Ekmek Kataifi	*186*
Flaky Coconut Pie	*190*
Ricotta Cheese Fruit Bake	*194*

Anginetti Lemon Cookies — *198*

Toasted Almond Biscotti — *202*

Greek Rice Pudding — *206*

Sauce — **209**

Tomato Sauce — *210*

Ancho Sauce — *212*

Miso Sauce — *214*

Chili Barbecue Sauce — *216*

Dressing — **219**

Emulsified French Dressing — *220*

Caesar Dressing — *222*

Cooked Salad Dressing — *224*

Low Fat Buttermilk Yogurt Dressing — *226*

Conclusion — **228**

Measurement Conversions — *229*

About the Author — *230*

References — *231*

Index — *232*

Printed in Great Britain
by Amazon